"For generations, influence was determined by who owned the press. In an age where everyone has that power via social networks, reputation managers must learn how to find, engage, and partner with the people shaping their brands. Schaefer provides unmatched insight into the newest ways to find who matters."

—**HAROLD BURSON,** Founder, Burson-Marsteller

"*Return on Influence* is an astoundingly fluid read thanks to Mark's conversational writing style. His profound insights on influence are shared via first-hand experiences as a world-class social media and marketing leader, interviews with influential leaders, relevant case studies and a deep dive into what Klout's all about. This book provides a path for understanding and optimizing influence as a positive force in your world, whether you're an innovative individual or a global brand."

—**BILLY MITCHELL,** President & Senior Creative Director, MLT Creative

"In the past, corporate and government leaders built strong networks of influence one relationship at a time. Mark Schaefer's latest book explains how today's social media stands that model on its end—enabling average citizens to create even more influential networks by the tens-of-thousands in a fraction of the time."

—**CHRIS PETERS,** CEO, The Lucrum Group

"In a world afflicted with 'continuous partial attention,' it's intellectually refreshing to read Mark W. Schaefer's clearly written *Return on Influence*. Determining influence in online and offline conversations, understanding the power and premise of social scoring, and connecting with niche influencers give a hint to the level of research invested in these twelve chapters. Communicators and CMOs will find Chapter 5 a game-changer. The ultimate influencer will harness the insight in Schaefer's book and leverage it for more and better business."

—**ANNE DEETER GALLAHER,** Owner/CEO, Deeter Gallaher Group LLC

ROI

RETURN ON INFLUENCE

ROI
RETURN ON INFLUENCE

THE REVOLUTIONARY POWER OF KLOUT, SOCIAL SCORING, AND INFLUENCE MARKETING

MARK W. SCHAEFER

New York Chicago San Francisco Lisbon London Madrid Mexico City
Milan New Delhi San Juan Seoul Singapore Sydney Toronto

For Rebecca, who demonstrates every moment, every day,
the only kind of influence that really matters.

CONTENTS

Influence in the Digital Age

By Lee Rainie,
Director, Pew Research Center's Internet & American Life Project

T he idea of influence is rooted in astrology. Some long-ago Gauls started using the word *influence* because they figured the reason people often acted as they did lay in the stars, which emanated a force that pushed our ancestors in one direction or another. It had to be that "inflow" of cosmic vibes that accounted for the weird way people reacted to things. Centuries later, of course, the idea of being "under the influence" took on a wholly different meaning.

Research in recent decades has taken a lot of the mumbo-jumbo and guesswork out of the study of influence. Indeed, it was a giant breakthrough in the mid-twentieth century when the scholars Paul Lazarsfeld, Elihu Katz, and their disciples theorized that influence emerges from a "two-step flow of communication." The idea was that "opinion leaders" filter information between the mass media and ordinary citizens, and it was their encounters with discussion among those elite "influentials" about new information that really drove the way citizens formed opinions and made decisions. The scholars' insight was that individuals are influenced more by the people with whom they interact than by the messages they get from mass media. It was a theory eagerly embraced by marketers, political practitioners, communications gurus, public health advocates, and those who study the dissemination of innovation and ideas.

One of the many disruptions caused by the digital age has been to the two-step theory. Mark Schaefer's original insights here are a testament to that. The digital disruption has not challenged a core tenet of two-step proponents that influence flows from encounters with others. But three revolutions in the digital space have brought new kinds of actors, new kinds of encounters, and new kinds of information into the influence marketplace.

The first revolution is the rise of the Internet, especially broadband connections. As we at the Pew Internet Project watched broadband being deployed into the homes of two-thirds of Americans, we saw a sharp increase in the number of people who created and shared information and media. These citizen publishers and broadcasters vastly broadened the number of media centers that were disseminating commercial information, health and medical material, political advocacy, hobbyist and do-it-yourself primers, lifestyle pointers, spiritual insights, and on and on and on. This is an unprecedented explosion of storytelling and, yes, of nodes of influence. Sometimes the influence is felt through individual interactions; at other times the sheer weight of anonymous crowds does the job. And "influentials" do not necessarily come with credentials. Amateur experts are much in evidence in every field. This book tells the story of many of them. Moreover, some of the most important new influencers in this world are machine algorithms that sort through all this digital content to try to make sense of it. Influence is embedded in Google's PageRank.

The second revolution is tied to the rise of mobile devices and mobile connections. At the moment I write, 84 percent of American adults and 80 percent of teenagers have cell phones, more than half of adults have laptops with mobile ties, and 11 percent have tablet computers. All told, 63 percent of adults connect to the Internet on the fly. Mobile connectivity has elevated the importance of just-in-time searches and real-time information and insight. As people's expectations about the availability of others and of information adjust to this always-on reality, influence is exercised in the tap on an app. Decisions and actions that depend on information exchanges can now be much more spur of the moment than in the past.

The third revolution relates to social networking sites themselves. Social networks (bunches of friends and acquaintances) have been around forever. But the rise of sites such as Facebook in the middle to late 2000s has changed information flows through networks and reconfigured influence inside networks. One of the ways in which people now cope with information overload is to rely more heavily on others in their social networks to alert them to news of all kinds (big cultural stuff as well as social tidbits), help them evaluate information that is confusing, and become consumers of information that is generated in social media. And in a broadband and mobile world, people create new advice-and-support networks with some regularity to tackle particular issues, for example, how to respond to a new ailment diagnosis or complete a car purchase.

Added up, the three revolutions and the changes in technology just around the corner have galvanized those who hope to understand the nature of influence. There are fortunes to be made and lives to be saved in analyzing the exabytes of data generated by humans and machines to determine how people allocate their attention, what messages make a difference as they decide what to do, which interventions through what channels change harmful behavior, and which past activities predict future actions. As exciting as that is to commercial and scholarly pursuers, I would sound a note of warning: If people feel stalked or misunderstood or manipulated as these explorations are under way, the whole enterprise will come crashing down. As Schaefer notes, this is the era of Citizen Influencers, and they will surely raise their powerful voices against those who exploit or mistreat them.

Assuming the research is done sensitively and correctly, it is likely that the insights will lead to conclusions that influence can be understood in the same way we are learning to understand disease. Now that human and germ genomes are available for study, the evidence shows that there usually are subtle interactions between genes and the environment that lead to illness. As influence is studied in the coming years, we could find there are similar subtle interactions between different types of people in different kinds of conditions (the gene side of the story) and different information inputs that come from different sources (the environment side of the story).

In other words, influence is distributed and context-dependent. That is one of the implicit narratives captured in the decade of research by the Pew Internet Project. People generally say that the best thing the digital revolution has given them is more of what they already want: more opportunity to communicate, more access to information, more capacity to learn at their own pace, more variety of sources of information, and more chances to find others with whom they can share something that interests them, such as ideas or passions. Of course, that means they have more opportunities to be influenced and to be influential. Hence, the story of this book.

I have become a number.

And if you are even slightly active on social media sites such as Twitter, Facebook, and LinkedIn, you have become a number too, at least in the eyes of a new breed of influence marketers. Our numbers are being compiled, sorted, sliced, diced, priced, dissected, combined, and filleted in ways that help companies sell more of their stuff.

If you are fortunate enough to have a number that is high, it might earn you a free gaming system, movie tickets, clothes, sports equipment, a vacation to Las Vegas or Europe.

If your number is low, you will receive nothing.

By the way, everybody knows everybody else's scores. They're posted for the world to see.

This trend of social scoring is creating new classes of haves and have-nots, social media elites and losers, frenzied attempts to crash the upper class, and deepening resentments.

Social scoring is also the centerpiece of an extraordinary marketing movement. For the first time, companies can—with growing confidence—identify, quantify, and nurture valuable word-of-mouth influencers who can uniquely drive demand for their products. This book demonstrates why these controversial developments are also historically important for business leaders.

Influence

The word *influence* used to be in the same "soft" category as *love*, *hate*, and *interested*. Now we're beginning to measure it? Don Draper and his Mad Men would have loved that!

I'm writing this book because I'm fascinated by this intersection of unprecedented business opportunity and extreme personal loathing.

Every time I write a blog post on the subject of social scoring, my readers foam at the mouth. "The only thing that stops me from taking this seriously is that I trust my fellow citizens to oppose this as vehemently as I do," one reader wrote. His passion sounded more like a political speech than the typical daily blog comment.

"Why don't you take a stand and help STOP this!" another reader demanded.

Stop it? Why would we want to, even if we could? What is so personally threatening about a simple ranking? After all, common Internet analytics programs already offer scads of data to determine the success of our online ads, websites, and blogs. It's no secret that Facebook and Google keep running accounts of our every move, want, and desire with a cold completeness and unnerving efficiency that would shock even George Orwell.

We know it's happening. We are rated and categorized constantly, and for the most part we resign ourselves to that fact. But there seems to be something dramatically different about this notion of social scoring that makes people spitting mad. When the number crunchers twist and turn that data to evaluate people, look out! This powerful business trend is tapping into something visceral and emotional that I have not seen before.

Social media platforms such as Twitter, Facebook, LinkedIn, and Google+ are upending the traditional concept of influence. Classical models of power are being flipped around in an Internet environment where nobody really knows who is who. In our dense world of daily communication tsunamis, people yearn to find shortcuts to truth, quick reads on power, and 140-character directives to make their lives easier. The trappings of social proof implied by the number of Twitter followers or Facebook "likes" may be more important signs of accomplishment to many people than a lifetime of real achievements. The consequences for those who seek online power and influence are vast.

If you have a social media account, you are already being judged. Companies with names like Klout, PeerIndex, and Twitter Grader are in the process of scoring millions, eventually billions, of people on their level of influence. And they're not simply looking at the number of followers or friends you've amassed. They are beginning to measure online influence through extraordinarily complex algorithms tweaked daily by teams of PhD-level researchers and scientists. They're declaring their judgments online, too, for the entire world to see.

Although being publicly rated and compared has a significant icky factor, we can't ignore the breathtaking business opportunities. When companies such as Disney, Nike, and Microsoft are creating successful marketing efforts centered on people's social influence scores, as a business professional, you'd better take that seriously. *In essence, these companies are leveraging an entirely new marketing channel based on widespread access to personal influence.*

The more success these brands have, the more swag they'll lavish on the new influence class and the hotter the fires of indignation will rage within those left behind. We are at the dawn of the creation of a new social media caste system determined by how and when you tweet, connect, share, and comment. The haves may score better jobs, higher social status, even better luck on the dating scene. The rules of personal power in our world have been changed forever. And there's no turning back.

How are you going to fare?

The good news is that in this new world of social influence, even the obscure, the shy, and the overlooked can become celebrities in their slice of the online world. You no longer have to win an election, be an elite athlete, or possess movie star looks to have power. We are entering the age of the Citizen Influencer, in which every person has a chance to get behind the velvet rope and be treated like a rock star. This is our time. This is *your* time.

You too can be an Internet celebrity.

You too can earn your way into the influence class.

You too can discover the power of your own return on influence. And in fact, many companies already have.

Let's begin.

Getting the Most Out of This Book

I know you are pretty excited about this book, but hold on one darn minute. I need to give you fair warning. You are about to enter a world of tweets, retweets, shares, likes, followers, and blogs. To get the most out of this book, it would be useful to have a general knowledge of the quirky terminology of social media. If you're already immersed in places such as Twitter, Facebook, and LinkedIn, proceed. You're going to have a lot of fun with *Return on Influence*!

If this territory is unfamiliar to you, this subject is still relevant because the trends and topics in this book are going to apply to everybody. But if you're thinking, What the heck's a tweet? I've prepared a little surprise for you. Appendix A is a social media primer that takes a look at the differences between traditional media channels such as television and newspapers and the new opportunities of social media marketing. That appendix also unravels some of the unfamiliar language of the social web that will help you enjoy the book even more. Appendix B provides a rundown of the most popular social scoring platforms.

If you're a social media newbie, take a moment to check out Appendixes A and B before proceeding. Go ahead, take a look. I'll wait for you!

ROI
RETURN ON INFLUENCE

The Roots of Influence

With more than 10 years' experience leading digital and interactive marketing programs at Fortune 500 companies and some of the world's biggest brands, Sam Fiorella has earned the right to walk into any job interview with a little swagger. But the professional marketer was stopped dead in his tracks during an interview when a manager from a global advertising firm asked him about his Klout score.

"I thought it was pretty good, a 45," he said. "But when I told him, the guy just got this look of disdain on his face and said, 'Oh, really,' and that was pretty much the end of the interview. When I didn't hear anything for a week, I followed up with him, and he told me my online influence was not sufficient for the job requirements."

Fiorella had learned about Klout, a company that dispenses personal influence ratings, at a business networking meeting a few weeks before. "People were comparing their scores," he said, "and I faked my way through by saying I hadn't checked mine in a while. But I immediately went home and looked it up."

That was Sam's introduction to social scoring, the process by which companies are compiling billions of individual online activities, assessing individual influence on various topics, and distilling your personal efforts and success to a single number.

Furious and more than a little concerned, Fiorella went on a tweeting rampage to increase his Klout score by any means. He was determined that his experience at the ad agency interview would never be repeated. He carefully studied and tried to reproduce the

1

online behaviors of top-rated influencers. When he spoke at conferences, he made sure that every slide had a "tweetable quote" aimed at the Klout algorithm and asked attendees to tweet his name throughout the presentation. He engineered his online engagement to attract the attention of high Klout influencers who could bend his score upward and filtered his followers by their levels of influence so that he knew which contacts to nurture to affect his score.

"I realized I was gaming the system," he said, "and I felt strange about that but thought I had to do this to be competitive in my industry. It looked like this was becoming an expectation of employment."

Within a few months, Sam had driven his score up to an elite level of 70 points, a gaudy score on a measurement platform where the average influence level is about 19. "I became obsessed with it," he said. "On any given day I could tell you my Klout score within half a point."

"I know it's insane," he said. "But even if it means nothing to me personally, it seems to mean something to everybody else whether I'm worthy of attention or not, whether I have something valuable to say or not. I'm just at a point now that if I can't beat 'em, I'll join 'em, and, well, I'll just have the highest Klout score that there ever was.

"It doesn't matter if it's accurate. It's a perception. So you have to deal with it."

■ ■ ■

After Valentina Monte accepts a date, the Boston University senior quickly goes online to see how many Twitter followers her suitor has. Online scoring certainly plays a much different role in her life. According to an account in the *Boston Globe* in February 2011, she checks her follower count three times a day. When she meets someone who admits to following more people than follow him, she judges: "That means you're a loser."

When her Klout score hit an impressive 59 out of 100 recently, she was ecstatic: "I felt worthy."

"I am genuinely on Twitter all of the time," she told me. "I don't remember how I functioned before." She has set up training programs for her sorority sisters to get them on board, too. "Looking to the future, I think this can be part of my professional development. I think it can be a point of differentiation," she said.

■ ■ ■

The Palms Hotel in Las Vegas has created a Klout Klub to provide online influencers with room upgrades and other benefits based on the numerical rating of their online influence on Twitter and Facebook.

■ ■ ■

Naveen Krishnamurthy is an Internet start-up veteran and president/
CEO of RIVA Solutions, Inc.

Judging a person's level of online influence has become a core
competency for Naveen and his company's business model. "When
I tried to recruit social media associates and strategists, I found that
9 out of 10 didn't really get it. There are a lot of posers out there. I
want to find the people who are online because they are knowledgeable, passionate, and excited about what they are doing. Looking at
a person's Klout score seems to be a good indicator of that, a good
way to recruit."

To help him network with potential employees and partners who
have online influence, Naveen helped create an exclusive club in his
area limited to people with Klout scores over 50 out of a possible
100. "It's fun to meet with people who 'get it,' " he said, "but I also
think this will serve as a source of new employees and resources for
my company."

Naveen believes strongly in the ability of these social scoring
developments to predict success in the workplace. "When I was coming up through the ranks, HR departments used the Myers-Briggs
test to gauge personality traits. I think these social scores could
eventually have the potential to grade employees on the likelihood
of their success in many jobs in the workplace today. So many jobs
depend on your ability to work in an Internet environment."

He encourages his employees to improve their online status
through friendly competition. Naveen recently sponsored a contest to
see who could have the biggest improvement in his or her Klout score,
with the winning employee being awarded a trip to Las Vegas. "And
by the way," he adds, "since we posted news about the contest, we've
had dozens of people contact us about working at our company!"

■ ■ ■

The company at the epicenter of this power quake is Klout, and its
employees see desperation on a daily basis. "People call and say,
'I work in social media, and I'm going to lose my job if my score
doesn't rise,'" one employee said in an *AdAge* magazine article. "We
get celebrity managers asking how they can get their clients' scores
higher. We get people who are literally crying because their Klout
score went down."

■ ■ ■

People are crying over some company's *made-up score*?

CHAPTER 1

The Rise of the Citizen Influencer

FlyingPhotog Paul Thompson
Just updated my resume to include my Klout score.
11 May 10

f you haven't heard of Klout and the emerging field of social influence measurement, you probably will soon as these measures wind their way into mainstream life. If you're active on Facebook, LinkedIn, Twitter, or YouTube, it's likely that your score is being assessed by a major company or brand right now whether you realize it or not.

Klout is one of a number of new status-measuring companies whose purpose is to curate billions of individual pieces of information, apply complex mathematical algorithms, and feed that information to businesses in ways that will create new marketing programs aimed at selling more of their skin care products, cars, and movies.

It's turning into big business, creating a new marketing gold rush. Some of the pioneers in the field characterize this new ability to identify word-of-mouth influencers as an important development in the history of business. For the first time, the world's biggest brands have a way to cost-effectively and rapidly identify, connect with, and nurture customers who are their megaconnectors in niche markets.

When Virgin America opened its Toronto route last spring, it asked Klout to find a small group of influencers to receive a free flight in hopes that they'd effectively spread the word. "We offered 120 free flights for this campaign—all of which were booked within a matter of weeks—so we were very pleased with how much enthusiasm was generated to take advantage of our offer," said Porter Gale, who was cited in *AdAge* and was then vice president of marketing at Virgin. "We saw a ton of social media buzz and press around the campaign, which definitely helped to build awareness for our brand and product in the Toronto market."

After the initial 120 participants and an additional 144 engaged influencers had been accrued, the word-of-mouth power kicked in as those highly social individuals generated more than 4,600 tweets about the new route. That led to more than 7.4 million impressions and coverage in top blogs and news outlets such as the *LA Times* and CNN. All it took was making those original 120 people feel special.

Think about it: 7.4 million impressions and coverage in top media outlets. That's hard, cold measurement for marketers, who are always struggling with the notion of building brand awareness. Those campaigns didn't depend on expensive celebrity spokespersons, Hollywood personalities, or sports stars. The platform has the potential to bring true celebrity status and all the associated perks to anyone who is willing to work for it. Anybody has a chance to experience life on the other side of the velvet rope.

Even Calvin Lee.

The Citizen Influencer

Lee, a graphic designer employed by the city of Los Angeles, may be the poster child for the new class of Citizen Influencer. He was one of the lucky ones on that free Virgin flight to Toronto simply because he is an authentically nice guy and a massive tweeter. "I'm addicted," he joked. "I really can't stop."

He's about as humble, quiet, and mild-mannered as any person you are likely to meet. When I interviewed him, it was difficult to get more than a few sentences out of him at a time. But in Twitterland, where success is defined on the basis of the ability to express oneself in just 140 characters at a time, the shy Lee has become a rock star.

"I've gone through life wondering what my 'thing' would be. I believe I've found it . . . well, more like it found me," he said. "Twitter is really what started it all for me. I've never thought of myself as being in social media. It kind of just happened. Now I love it."

Lee, who describes himself in his Twitter profile as a "social media ho," has become a human news service. "I tweet at least 200 times a day," he said. "Anything that interests me: food, travel, entertainment.

And of course design and social media. I look for interesting links from my friends and sift through them for good stuff I like. I love engaging with my community. I try to be a resource for them. I share what I enjoy in my life, and I'm very transparent about everything I do. I tweet photos from my life and talk about things I enjoy. I think people feel that I am a real person and part of their lives."

He has apparently been quite successful, amassing nearly 80,000 followers on Twitter. But more important, it is a highly engaged audience whose members seem to appreciate his work . . . for the most part. "I have a few haters," he said. "People who say I tweet too much or whatever. But that's the beauty of Twitter. There is always that unfollow button!"

Like any good networker, Calvin Lee frequently moves his online relationships into offline friendships, especially by attending conferences. I first met Calvin at the South by Southwest Conference, an annual event in Austin, Texas, that frequently is described as spring break for geeks. It's also the place to see and be seen for the Twitterati. He was instantly recognizable by his wide grin and the shock of porcupine-like black hair poking from the top of his head.

"I was not very popular in high school," he continued. "But now I'm like the big jock on campus. It's amazing. I can walk around a big conference, and everybody seems to know me. I've even been recognized just walking down the street."

When Lee tweets, people respond, and his growing influence has won him celebrity-status perks. In addition to the free airline ticket, brands have reached out to him and provided

- A brand-new Audi A8 to test-drive for a week
- Hundreds of dollars in gift cards from American Express, Timbuk2, and other brands
- A pass to the House of Blues VIP event at the private Las Vegas Foundation Room club
- A free Samsung Focus smartphone and an invitation to the launch party for the device
- Flight, hotel, and meals to attend an exclusive conference featuring speakers from Facebook, Foursquare, and Zynga
- Eight passes to the VH1 Do Something Awards, where he hobnobbed with Hollywood celebrities

Calvin Lee doesn't have the trademark characteristics of a celebrity influencer, does he? He doesn't exert his power through

TV spots or news interviews. He's not an accomplished musician, athlete, actor, or politician. Calvin doesn't live in a mansion in the Hollywood Hills. He doesn't have an Ivy League degree; he went to a trade school and attended a community college.

But he's massively present on the social web. On average, he is sharing some piece of content every five minutes, 24 hours a day, 365 days a year. Calvin is nice to people. He helps his followers in any way he can and tries humbly to provide value with the information he shares. "Building a following on Twitter is like providing great customer service," he said. "I'm always there to help a friend, charities, and my community."

He also helps create positive content about the brands that are connecting with him, and that content hums and buzzes throughout his vast network and beyond.

"An extra bonus of all this sharing and helping is that it somehow created influence and trust for me. Brands have been reaching out to me, sending me on trips and asking me to try their goods and services, and they want me to review their products. I'm not sure that would have happened without the exposure I got through Klout," he contends.

Lee knows that to stay in that rarefied air of being the everyman of celebrities, he has to keep his presence and his content sharing at a very high level. "I do feel some pressure. I got to this level, and I don't want to slip. So I'm always tweeting at my work breaks . . . even on vacation. I never stop."

But the new influencers don't even need a massive number of followers or years of experience on Twitter. They just have to make things happen.

Take Charles Dastodd, for example. He has less than 5 percent of Calvin Lee's followers. On the list of the most followed people in Chicago, he doesn't even crack the top 1,000. But as the *Chicago Tribune* reported, Dastodd is among the top 10 social media influencers in the city.

He uses Twitter, Facebook, and Flickr to promote his unique photography and provide an escape from his doctoral work in the humanities at the University of Chicago. But when he tweets about photography, people respond. He started getting requests for event and portrait photography from his followers and messages from photographers seeking advice on starting a business or improving their portfolios.

That kind of influence was detected by the social scoring algorithms at Klout, and he was approached to attend a celebrity event at the Museum of Contemporary Art in Chicago exclusively for people with high Klout scores.

From now on, you don't have to be George Clooney or Lady Gaga to get an invitation to the exclusive world behind the velvet rope. We're at the dawn of a new era of the democratization of influence.

This concept is revolutionary. Or maybe, in a way, we're returning to the very roots of influence: conversations between real people that make something happen.

After all, the first markets were conversations, simple places where people gathered to exchange information and goods: a city market or a town square. Supply met demand with a firm handshake. Buyers and sellers looked each other in the eye, met, and spoke directly to one another without the filter of media executives, the manipulation of marketing, the arrogance of advertising, or the positioning of public relations. People bought and sold goods and services to people they knew and trusted.

There is a lot of buzz about social media ushering in this new age of conversation. This is untrue, of course: The conversation was always there. We just couldn't find it because it was interrupted for a few decades by the introduction of broadcast media. Social media platforms allow us to start to reclaim the conversation with our customers, even in a complex global marketplace.

Marketing, Interrupted

Beginning with radio and then TV, companies discovered the efficiency of moving from selling goods such as soap, cereal, and bread through local producers to manufacturing in bulk and marketing through mass media. Undoubtedly it worked, and still does, with powerful efficiency. But at the same time, the conversations were happening without the benefit of the local marketplace. Influence was obscured or pushed into homes and suburban neighborhoods. Success was measured by advertising "impressions," assuming that those impressions were going to hit at least some of the right people at some of the right times.

In that era, approximations for market conversations had to be created. This was the golden age of polling and focus groups. We had to *create* conversations when we lost touch with the community marketplace.

The Conversation Renaissance

In 1999, a seminal and visionary book, *The Cluetrain Manifesto,* was published. Authors Christopher Locke, Doc Searls, David Weinberger, and Rick Levine saw that this emerging Internet technology could help us recapture those historic market conversations, as it stated:

> *In the early 1990s, there was nothing like the Internet we take for granted today. Back then, the Net was primitive, daunting, uninviting. So what did we come for? And the answer is: each other. The Internet became a place where people could talk to other people without constraint. Without filters or censorship or official sanction—and perhaps most significantly, without advertising.*

When *Cluetrain* was written, there were just 50 million people on the Internet, most of them with AOL dial-up accounts. And yet it correctly foretold the potential for mass conversation, the opportunities for influence, and the inherent fear traditional advertisers would have of giving up control of the dialogue.

The market conversation that became lost in the mass media megaphone was found again in quiet discussions in geeky chat rooms and news exchanges on the first Internet sites.

Conversation as god

Within 10 years of the publication of *The Cluetrain Manifesto,* two trends collided that not only reenergized the idea of conversation but elevated it to superstar status. The first was a critical mass of diverse demographic categories actually accessing and using the Internet. The web went free, fast, and global.

The second was the emergence of user-friendly, enjoyable, and helpful sharing sites that collectively became known as social media. This allowed people to connect, comment, and publish quickly and easily. For the first time in history, our civilization could conduct free, global, instantaneous conversations. It was momentous. Now when companies spoke, people started talking back!

Everybody became a publisher: customers, suppliers, and employees; community members and activists; people who loved you and people who hated you.

They contributed videos, blogs, comments, updates, tweets, music, art, reviews, photos—every imaginable type of content, billions of pieces of it every hour of the day. And your company had better be in tune with it. The idea of influence hit hyperdrive. As one marketer friend put it, "The deer now have guns!"

The popularity of social platforms naturally attracted large corporations, advertisers, and search engine optimization (SEO) alchemists. By 2009, companies both large and small had joined the social media frenzy, trying to make sense of the unprecedented amount of direct consumer information that was flooding the airwaves.

Sophisticated listening programs emerged that could slice and dice consumer sentiment, monitor competitor activities, detect shifts and trends, excavate potential problems, and, perhaps most important, begin to link consumer online activity with market influence.

Driven by the belief that a recommendation from a friend or trusted peer carries more weight than an impersonal advertisement, brands were eager to find consumers who could motivate others in their online spheres to take action or try a new product. This realm of social media marketing is potentially lucrative for companies seeking fresh ways to reach potential customers who are spending more of their lives online. Identifying and connecting with Citizen Influencers became paramount for many brands. Not being part of the conversation can be perilous.

A New Kind of Conversation

Here's an example of this new kind of customer conversation in action.

My wife and I decided to celebrate for no particular reason and go out to a favorite restaurant we had not visited in at least six months. We were seated at our table promptly.

When my wife went to the restroom and I wanted to pass some time, I checked into this restaurant by using the Foursquare application on my smartphone. Foursquare is a useful tool that allows you to view deals and reviews at just about any location you could visit and even see if you have any friends nearby.

When I checked into this location, I was surprised and delighted to see a review from one of my best friends pop up on my screen. What a coincidence. He had been to the same restaurant just that week. Here is his review:

This restaurant has always been a family favorite but the service has really gone downhill. I'm convinced the management and staff don't even care anymore.

Wow. My friend is a very kind and patient man, so the service must have been absolutely horrible for him to leave a review like that!

My wife returned to the table, and after 10 minutes we still didn't have anybody take our drink order. Normally, I would have been engaging in conversation with my wife and probably not even noticing the delay, but now my Spidey senses seemed to be tuned fully to the service level.

It occurred to me that I was now *expecting* poor service because of my friend's review. Whether we had a good waiter or not, I was closely watching for signs of problems.

"Don't you think the service here is slow tonight?" I asked.

"Well, maybe," my wife responded. "But I've noticed that the waiter had a lot of tables getting their food at the same time, so I think this is probably normal."

She had not received the same influential message I had, and so she had a totally different experience with the restaurant. She was looking forward to a nice meal at a bustling restaurant. I was looking forward to slow service.

This is how the power of an online influencer can work for or against a business at any moment. I had not seen my friend or spoken to him about the restaurant, yet his power was extending beyond space and time to me and who knows how many others. This is a new kind of conversation, isn't it? Asynchronous, permanent, searchable, and powerful.

An advertising image may be fleeting and ignored. A television commercial is viewed with suspicion. But a Citizen Influencer like my friend can have a long-lasting influence in his or her sphere of connection and engagement with just two sentences of original content.

This example also illustrates the role of social media and the influence it enables as a rapid catalyst for change, service, and continuous improvement. If the restaurant had been attentive to my friend in the first place, it never would have received that negative review. It's possible that the manager doesn't even know the review exists, and if the restaurant doesn't address any of the core problems it is experiencing, the reviews will continue to pile up to the point where it won't know what hit it. Customers will pick up on the negative buzz on places like Foursquare, Yelp, and Urbanspoon and simply stay away.

Social media is like a Darwinian hypercatalyst. Businesses better adapt, adopt, and become the fittest because the societal pressures through self-publishing and reviews like this are unprecedented.

With the near ubiquity of smartphones, the Internet surrounds us. If I had seen the review before I entered the restaurant, maybe I would have avoided it altogether.

Conversation and Influence

Valentina Monte's recent experience with a Klout-related gift from Subway restaurants demonstrates the other side of social content generation: the opportunity for positive influence.

The Boston student was thrilled when she received her first free gift because of her high Klout score. Klout is the leading company attempting to quantify the influence of social media users though a single score.

"I learned about Klout from an advertising industry publication last year," she said. "I became really interested in this because I can see how it can relate to my future profession. I knew that businesses sometimes sent you free stuff if you have a high score, but I never considered that it would happen to me. So I was surprised when I received a $10 Subway gift card to try a new turkey avocado sandwich.

"When I received the card in the mail, I tweeted about it. I even took a picture of the card and tweeted that too! Then I tweeted again when I got the actual sandwich and took a picture of it and sent that to my friends. I checked in on Foursquare when I was at the Subway restaurant. And all this time my friends are also tweeting back, telling me how cool it is. I can see why it makes a lot of sense to a brand because it's just free PR for them. I'm just a very social person in this space anyway, so I wasn't doing anything different from the normal for me."

Subway's investment in Valentina and her influence was a good one.

More than 20 pieces of positive content were created during her one visit to a Subway store. The reach? Valentina has more than 2,000 followers, but who knows for sure? Tweeting is a little like throwing a message in a bottle into the ocean. A positive review on Foursquare lasts indefinitely, just as the negative one did.

The point is that Subway didn't have to use NASCAR driver Jeff Gordon or even Jared the healthy sandwich guy to tell their story. They didn't spend millions producing and airing television ads. The story of their new sandwich was being told by thousands of people—Citizen Influencers—in the moment, organically, in their stores, by people actually eating their sandwiches.

Nish Weiseth, who publishes a popular blog called *The Outdoor Wife*, is having a global impact through her content.

"I started blogging about a year and a half ago," she said. "I was in the throes of postpartum depression, and I needed an outlet. I was already writing a bit in my journal, and a lot of my writings were actually rather creative. So I decided to start posting them.

"I approach the blog as a dialogue between myself and others. As we get to know each other and expand our conversations, trust and respect is built. That's attractive to people, and others jump in. I just like to be honest about life, faith, and what's going on in the world. Honesty usually creates good content.

"Recently, I was asked to travel to Bolivia with World Vision along with a group of very influential bloggers. The purpose of the trip was to expose us to World Vision's work in child sponsorship through meeting families and visiting programs and communities. We then blogged about our experience each day. Through the collaborative effort from each of our blogs, we've managed to get over 150 children sponsored. Being a part of that was really powerful."

Nish may not be receiving an Audi to drive for the weekend or an invitation to a movie premiere, but she is unquestionably influencing people to take action through her content. The bits of technology enabling that possibility were not in place even a few years ago. She is taking advantage of an opportunity to connect and influence globally that is unprecedented in the history of humankind, and you can too.

The Once and Future Conversation

Has the social web reconnected the consumer conversation? Has technology reestablished a medieval sense of knowing your customer to the point of anticipating needs? Has the ability to create content—a review, a tweet, a blog post—turned the idea of power on its head?

This book will open your mind to the new rules of power and influence on the social web. Through the voices and experiences of the dozens of experts who helped create this book, it will shift the way you think about your personal power, the ability to leverage the power of others, and the importance of the new class of Citizen Influencers to the world of marketing and advertising.

So let's dig a little deeper now and begin our journey. What does it mean to be an influencer anyway, and how has the social web changed this concept forever?

CHAPTER 2

Igniting Epidemics

Scobleizer Robert Scoble
@OWStarr I am lurking on Quora, but not answering much
lately. I should jump back in.
2 Oct

Amy Howell ignites epidemics. In a good way, of course.
Epidemics of excitement. Epidemics of business connections. Epidemics of influence.

Amy is a successful businessperson, the founder and
president of Memphis-based Howell Marketing, and is consistently
named as one of the most influential women on Twitter. She collects
business connections the way other folks collect rare toys or recipes.

When I interviewed her for this book, she was driving from her
vacation home to pick up a new friend in Nashville, Jessica Northey,
a prominent music industry blogger and promoter. Amy and Jessica
had exchanged a few Twitter messages before but had never met in
real life. When Amy heard that Jessica was in the state to do some
promotions for the country music industry, she drove three hours
out of her way to meet her. "I just decided to run up there and see
her," Amy said. "I thought it would be fun to meet her face-to-
face, and now I have this great new connection in the broadcasting
industry."

Jessica probably didn't realize it, but she had just been added to
Amy's collection.

In the world of influence marketing, Amy is a superconnector.
When people talk about six degrees of separation, if Amy is in the
mix, there are probably only three. She has built a substantial, successful business on the basis of her ability to connect with people in
extraordinary ways.

After graduating from college, Amy worked at a national accounting firm as its marketing director. "We were constantly trying to find ways to connect to new business opportunities," she said, "so I thought, Why don't we do that by helping other business professionals connect? I started a networking group and hosted it in our office—a roundtable lunch, an informal, nonstructured setting where all we did was talk about business issues in our region. It got to be pretty well known, and soon I became friends with 10 or 12 bright people who are real leaders in our city. We kind of grew up together, and many of them are still my friends and supporters today."

Amy had started her collection.

Over time, she built up enough powerful business relationships that she could launch her own PR and marketing firm. And then she found Twitter, a social media site in which people keep in touch and share information in 140-character bursts.

On Twitter she found a new platform to create connections far beyond her west Tennessee home. Business professionals from around the nation seemed to enjoy seeing her online each night, cutting up and offering help and advice. In a highly efficient manner and in the comfort of her office or home, she was able to extend the scope and depth of her collection like never before.

When Amy announced that she was hosting a social media networking event in Memphis, more than a dozen of her Twitter friends came from across the country—Texas, Georgia, New York, Pennsylvania—to meet her and, through her, meet one another face-to-face. I was one of those folks. Even though I had committed to speak at a national conference in Indianapolis the following day and would have to drive all night to attend Amy's event and uphold that commitment, I did it. Near the end of my fourteenth hour in the car over two days, I marveled that Amy had the power—the influence—to pull this off. There aren't too many family members I would have made that drive for, and this was somebody I knew only through Twitter? It made me think about the power of this tool to create not just relationships but movements, in this case a movement that was just beginning.

With Amy as its catalyst, the cross-country "tweet-up" generated powerful new friendships and business alliances. The group members realized they had enough synergy among them to create a virtual marketing agency that could have influence across the United States and Canada. A collaborative book project was launched, employment opportunities were created, and several significant new business partnerships emerged.

The group (or "the crew," as Amy started to call us) decided that this was just too much fun and decided to meet again a year later. I offered to host the meeting on the other side of the state in my home of Knoxville. With the help of Amy and an incredible team of volunteers, I created an event around the meeting of these 12 friends called Social Slam, which was attended by 430 people from 17 states. The attendees found the conference entirely by word of mouth—not a dime of advertising money was spent. We sold out weeks before the opening of the conference and probably could have sold 600 tickets. Buoyed by this initial success (and postevent feedback showing a 95 percent satisfaction level with the conference), we decided to make this an annual event. (Come next year, won't you?)

Amy had created an epidemic. She engineered small, weak connections on Twitter into dramatic action and powerful, lasting bonds that continue to touch thousands of people through the Social Slam legacy.

Amy, along with many people like her, represents the powerful word-of-mouth influencers, the new class of Citizen Influencers who can use the Internet to ignite epidemics across a state, a country, even the world.

These powerful influencers can move their friends in extraordinary ways and have long been the coveted and elusive targets of brands hoping for word-of-mouth product recommendations. But finding and connecting with these folks has been difficult and expensive.

Igniting Epidemics

In Malcolm Gladwell's acclaimed book *The Tipping Point*, he explains how these social epidemics are driven by the efforts of a handful of ultraconnecters like Amy Howell: sociable, energetic, knowledgeable people. Even mass marketing like television is truly effective only if it eventually ignites epidemics through this influence class. Gladwell writes:

> *Word of mouth is—even in this age of mass communications and multimillion dollar advertising campaigns—still the most important form of human communication. Think, for a*

moment, about the last expensive restaurant you went to, the last expensive piece of clothing you bought, and the last movie you saw. In how many of those cases was your decision about where to spend your money heavily influenced by the recommendation of a friend? There are plenty of advertising executives who think that precisely because of the sheer ubiquity of marketing efforts these days, word of mouth appeals have become the only kind of persuasion that most of us respond to anymore.

Yet, Gladwell says, word of mouth has remained mysterious. People share information among themselves all the time, but it's only in rare instances that such an exchange ignites a word-of-mouth epidemic.

I loved the example from the American Revolution that Gladwell described in his book. Gladwell uses the patriot Paul Revere as a dramatic example of the contrast between the power of influential superconnectors and that of the rest of us.

Revere had been tipped off that the British were planning an invasion and decided that communities surrounding Boston had to be warned. He jumped on a horse and began his midnight ride to Lexington. In two hours, he covered 13 miles. In every town he passed through he knocked on doors, informing local colonial leaders of the oncoming British and telling them to spread the word to others. Church bells started ringing. Drums started beating. The news spread like a virus as those informed by Paul Revere sent out riders of their own, until alarms were going off throughout the entire region. By 5 a.m. the word had reached 40 miles beyond his starting point.

When the British finally began their march, their foray into the countryside was met—to their astonishment—with fierce resistance. In the town of Concord, the British were confronted and soundly beaten by the colonial militia, and from that battle came the war known as the American Revolution.

But that's only half the story. At the same time Revere began his ride north of Boston, a fellow revolutionary named William Dawes set out on the same urgent errand to the towns west of Boston. But Dawes's ride never set the countryside afire. He had the same mission, but the local militia leaders weren't alerted.

If it were only the news itself that mattered in a word-of-mouth epidemic, Dawes would now be as famous as Paul Revere. He isn't. So why did Revere succeed where Dawes failed? The answer,

Gladwell states, is that the success of any kind of social epidemic is heavily dependent on the involvement of people with a particular and rare set of social gifts.

Paul Revere was a connector. He was gregarious and intensely social and seemed to be at the center of events from city planning to politics and from charity drives to hunting parties and the arts. He was a member of five political parties. Paul Revere was everywhere and knew everybody.

And William Dawes? He clearly had none of the social gifts of Revere, because there is almost no record of anyone who even remembers him that night. Dawes was in all likelihood a man with a normal social circle, which means that like most of us, once he left his hometown, he probably didn't know whose door to knock on.

That's the insight the world's biggest companies and brands are trying to mine from social media data. Who are their brands' Reveres and who are the Daweses? Who are the most knowledgeable, passionate, and connected people to put out the word about their brand and help it spread like wildfire? If you had the ability to find and connect with those people, wouldn't that be marketing gold? As we'll see, that's what companies such as Klout and PeerIndex are trying to accomplish with their complex algorithms.

Influence and Information Density

Of course, in today's world, Paul Revere could have gotten his message out on Facebook, Twitter, and YouTube or Renren in China, Mixi in Japan, and Vkontakte in Russia. From there it could have spread to traditional media outlets and reached millions more in less than the time it took him to ride to the towns and villages north of Boston that night. Today's igniters have access to virtually free, global, and certainly instantaneous communications systems.

Another difference is that in Revere's day, there was less complexity in the decision process. The act of being influenced was more straightforward than what we face today, immersed as we are in the density of modern life. New England at that time was probably the best-educated region on earth. In just over 50 years, the literacy rate in the northernmost colonies had risen from 50 percent to 90 percent by the time of the American Revolution.

Within Greater Boston there were no fewer than 10 newspapers at the time of the famous midnight ride. Even though this was one of the most educated, literate, and media-rich places on earth, a knock on the door from Paul Revere was probably still the most effective way to get a message to spread virally and quickly. Quite a contrast to our modern world, where the average American is bombarded with 108 advertising messages from TV, 34 from radio, and 112 from print sources every day, not to mention the total of 294 billion e-mails and 19 billion text messages radiating from our computers, smartphones, and iPads.

Evidence suggests that this crush of data and the ever-accelerating pace of modern life are creating automatic, mindless compliance in people, a willingness to say yes without thinking first. People can fall victim to the pull of the influence process in their everyday lives more easily and frequently.

Dr. Robert Cialdini, an author and researcher who has devoted much of his career to studying influence, explains: "In any situation where information is so dense and overwhelming, the irony is that there's so much information that it becomes irrelevant to the choice. We then have to revert to more primitive ways of deciding about what to do in a situation. We use these heuristics of badges, these rules of thumb which normally steer us correctly but may not suffice in all situations, because we just don't have the resources to fully examine all of the valuable data. It's just not possible anymore. So we go to these shortcuts."

The implication is that many people are more easily influenced by trustworthy friends because it is a useful shortcut in the daily decision-making process. Tweets and Facebook status updates have become a path to living your life in sound-bite-size chunks. It is little wonder that increasing proportions of corporate marketing budgets are now dedicated to creating content and encouraging interactions that may capture a share of that conversation. In fact, a common metric among the largest brands today is share of conversation, data distilled from powerful and sophisticated listening platforms finely tuned into the global sentiment. Companies such as Pepsi and McDonald's have war rooms set up to monitor global online conversation hot spots, respond to complaints, and identify trends.

Bringing the Pee-Wee Heat

This type of consumer autoresponse to authority is now ubiquitous in small ways too. One day, a prominent Twitter celebrity was kind enough to retweet one of my blog posts: Pee-wee Herman. Yes, I know, you're probably jealous. I'm sure you'll get over it.

Pee-wee's tweet resulted in a viral big adventure for my blog and nearly melted my servers. In fact, the website actually crashed for a while. Yet people continued to tweet the link even though they could not possibly have read the article when the servers were down because of the Pee-wee heat. Dozens of people were on autopilot, tweeting my blog post sight unseen—and certainly unread—simply because of the implied trust and influence of the person sending the tweet. Those folks were automatically advocating me, my brand, and my blog to untold others, probably without even knowing who I was or what I was writing about.

In the real world, can you imagine recommending a movie without seeing it? A restaurant without experiencing the food and service? A book without reading it? Yet these little shortcuts take place on the web constantly because the social media links are comparatively weak and the impact is so low. Whether it's a recommendation on a new restaurant or advice on a new smartphone application, the ability to rely on shorthand recommendations from our tribe of trusted advisors is becoming inexorably integrated into our culture. It's even influencing many traditional offline institutions.

Twenty years ago, if I wanted to hone my marketing skills or learn new business methods, I really had no choice: It was off to the classroom. There was no flood of Twitter links or blog posts, no online webinars. I would have to sit in a classroom or read a book and learn. But this expectation of autoresponse—this cultural conditioning to expect sound bites of information to help in making decisions—is also transferring to the real world.

"When I go to conferences now, people come up to me and want to know how to implement a marketing strategy in A, B, C steps," said Steve Farnsworth of Jolt Social Media, a Bay Area consulting company. "They want a marketing strategy in a tweet. Well, almost every marketing question should be answered with 'it depends,' but a lot of people don't want to take that time to really learn the answer. They just want to know how to do it in 30 minutes or less. They want to know the three main points and move on. They don't have time to learn or at least don't seem to have the priority to learn in an effective way."

That expectation will undoubtedly increase as an entire generation is learning to move through life by rapidly assimilating data in small, searchable bits, usually through a cell phone. Within a few years, smartphones will be the predominant "first screen" access to the Internet. It's already happening in Egypt, where 70 percent of the residents use a smartphone as their first point of access to the Internet.

By definition, we will be served smaller and smaller portions of information to make our daily decisions, if for no other reason than that the screens are so much smaller than even that of a laptop computer. As web development professionals optimize Internet-based information for the tiny screen, the first rule is to simplify—eliminate the details.

Influence on Autoresponse

The implication for our personal and work lives is vast. An entire generation has been conditioned to communicate, shop, search, learn, play, and manage their relationships through text messages. They are accustomed to the constant, gentle drip-drip-drip reward system of video games. Even e-mails are too long for the autoresponse crowd. A number of studies show that e-mail is all but dead for anybody under age 19.

"This trend of autoresponse to perceived authority is something I'm concerned about," said Jason Falls, founder of Social Media Explorer. "We trust information without doing due diligence or research and then pass along inaccurate or even deceptive information to our networks. I worry about that more than ever as spammers look for more creative ways to game the system and dupe us in a damaging and exponential form. There are people we allow to influence us that we don't have close personal ties to or long experience with, and that is dangerous. Bloggers and curators of content are especially vulnerable. We need to develop a higher litmus test so that our focus is on maintaining trust."

This ability to create autoresponse behaviors through influencers extends far beyond the Pee-tweeting episode. It can affect entire business models. Let's take a look at a recent example of a company's fortunes changing with a single blog post.

Quora and Scobleization

From its beginning, Quora was a company to watch. Founded by Facebook developer Charlie Cheever and Adam D'Angelo, Facebook's well-connected CTO and VP of engineering, this startup had a pedigree that demanded—and received—attention.

The business proposition was simple: create a sort of Wikipedia of answers to people's questions. The company describes its free product as "a continually improving collection of questions and answers created, edited, and organized by everyone who uses it. . . . By using Quora to document the world around them, our users are creating a database of knowledge that should grow and improve until almost everything that anyone wants to know is easily available in the system. When knowledge is put into Quora, it is there forever to be shared with anyone in the future who is interested."

But this was more than a question and answer forum. An engaging feature was the ability for participants to "vote up" or "vote down" answers, creating an environment that both rewarded the fittest answers and self-regulated against spam.

The company enjoyed early success and witnessed double-digit growth in use each quarter of its first year of operation. But as you can see in the chart below, something dramatic occurred in the waning days of 2010.

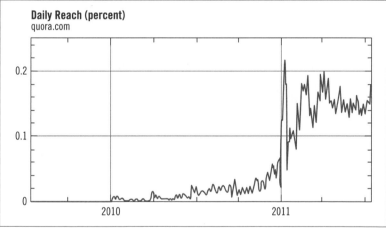

© 2011, Alexa Internet (www.alexa.com)

Quora had been Scobleized.

Robert Scoble probably exemplifies the power of social media to create Citizen Influencers better than any other human being on earth. Robert doesn't just move his 200,000 Twitter followers, 5,000 YouTube subscribers, and 5,000 Facebook fans to action; he moves markets.

After attending journalism school, Scoble fed his lifelong love of photography by taking a job in a San Jose camera shop. As a young man, he moved though a number of professional communication and video production positions before accepting the job that ignited his celebrity. In 2003, he joined Microsoft as part of the MSDN video team, where he produced and starred in videos that showcased Microsoft employees and products.

His geeky intellect and easygoing style made him an effective interviewer, but the fact that he also frequently criticized his own employer and praised competitors such as Apple and Google elevated him to cult hero. In these early days of blogs and social media, Scoble influenced a generation of bloggers and set a social media cultural tone with his direct approach and transparent communication style. He was friendly and accessible, even to the point of publishing his cell phone number on his blog. Robert Scoble may have become the world's first professional spokesblogger.

The Economist magazine described Scoble's influence in a 2005 profile: "He has become a minor celebrity among geeks worldwide, who read his blog religiously. Impressively, he has also succeeded where small armies of more conventional public-relations types have been failing abjectly for years: he has made Microsoft, with its history of monopolistic bullying, appear marginally but noticeably less evil to the outside world, and especially to the independent software developers that are his core audience."

In 2006 Scoble created a ripple in the technology industry when he left Microsoft. "Somebody leaked the story," he said. "It started to spread like wildfire. The story was pushed and doubled and went viral, and within three days, I had 15 million media impressions that all came from that one leak. It hit CNN, *Newsweek*, and the *New York Times*. My career never had had any momentous steps really. It was more like the frog that is being boiled slowly! But when this happened, I thought, Wow, this is pretty cool, and I certainly realized something was going on. I knew it would be a big story but didn't realize how big. I knew I was starting to get attention."

He began a series of career moves that leveraged his popularity and, more important, his access. His fame as an intellect and technology pundit made him a highly sought-after speaker and panelist at the most prestigious conferences and an A-list invitee for anybody trying to get attention for a new technology or start-up. He was invited to private parties of the tech elite, Space Shuttle launches, and government think tanks.

Scoble's ability to influence the behavior of his followers was probably never so well documented as in the events that occurred between December 26, 2010, and January 30, 2011. On a day when most people were enjoying holiday leftovers or shopping for postholiday sales, Robert wrote a blog post titled "Is Quora the Biggest Blogging Innovation in 10 Years?"

The post was a seven-point manifesto proclaiming Quora an improvement over blogging that incorporated the best elements of Twitter, Facebook, and social bookmarking sites. "I find that there's something addictive about participating [on Quora] instead of here on my blog," he wrote. "Why? Because when you see people voting up your answers or adding their own replies in real time it makes you realize there's a good group of people reading your stuff. I don't get that immediate rush here."

The response was profound. One man, through one blog post, had created the equivalent of a social media gold rush. Quora was the next big thing. A replacement for blogging. The place to see and be seen. The big buzz. Account registrations skyrocketed, servers sizzled, and within one week, the website's traffic had increased by nearly 400 percent. (At the time, I didn't see the big deal, which prompted one of my favorite blog post headlines: "Let's Not Have a Quor-gasm." This has nothing to do with the story. I just liked that headline. Thanks for obliging me. Now, back to our regularly scheduled programming.)

Robert's experience, access, and insight put him in a position to anticipate the company's success. "I probably get a lot more credit than I deserve," he said. "I see myself as somebody who has talent in doubling pennies. If you double a penny every day for a month, you are going to end up with a million dollars at the end of the month. The thing is, while it's true that most of Quora's growth happened in the three days after I published my article, I had put myself in front of that curve. I was watching things and saw that Quora was in that doubling mode, so when I finally jumped on board, it looked like I was responsible. Sure, I probably moved it along a little faster, but in a sense, I just jumped in front of the parade."

Scoble proved he was at the top of his game. Quora was soaring. His influence was at its peak. And then, in a matter of days, the unthinkable happened.

Robert changed his mind.

In his blog post titled "Why I Was Wrong about Quora as a Blogging Service . . ." published just one month after the initial missive that had ignited the Quora epidemic, he wrote, "Turns out I was totally wrong. It's a horrid service for blogging, where you want to put some personality into answers. It's just fine for a QA site, but we already have lots of those and, in fact, the competitors in this space are starting to react."

Traffic on Quora plummeted by more than 50 percent, nearly down to pre-Scobleized levels. Response to the about-face was harsh and swift, as typified by this entry on (where else?) Quora:

> *So Robert Scoble, it seems you don't like the heat. In the bygone days of what feels like ten minutes ago, you, the ubiquitous tech evangelist, larger-than-life personality and blogger, couldn't stop gushing about how great Quora was. Was Quora, you asked in the halcyon age of last December, the biggest blogging innovation in 10 years? Of course it was. Back in them days and throughout January, you could post answers to a wide range of questions and your ardent Twitter followers could up-vote them en masse and each up-vote and congratulatory comment could generate that awesome squirt of dopamine in your brain. Wasn't it grand?*

This was a lesson that our historic celebrity influencers know all too well. Simply being in the spotlight makes you a target. And being thrust into the new role of Citizen Influencer is no different.

Connecting Influence and Offline Behavior

Robert Scoble will be fine, I think. He continues to create great content through his blog, videos, and speaking appearances. The Scoble effect is alive and well, and just a mention on his blog or a video can double or triple traffic to a website in a single day. It is a concrete example of online influence driving behavior and results.

That's a hot debate. What good is measuring influence if we can't conclusively tie it to offline behavior? Amy Howell? Yeah, she can make people drive 14 hours to attend her conference. Paul Revere? Sure. He helped start a revolution. Pee-wee Herman? Well, maybe that's a bad example, but I think you are starting to see my point: Tying online behavior to offline results is dicey, at least right now.

We were lucky with this Quora example because a probable view of cause and effect is provided through data. Over the Christmas holiday of 2010–2011 it's unlikely that there were other significant confounding factors that could have created this instant groundswell of interest in a start-up social media site.

We'll look at this debate a little later in the book, but it provides a tantalizing view of the potential to tap into Citizen Influencers, doesn't it?

So let's spend a little time now exploring the nature of influence. What does it take to become a Citizen Influencer like Robert Scoble who can move hundreds or even thousands of people to take action? What's different about influence in the online world as opposed to the offline world, and how can you put it to work for you?

CHAPTER 3

The New Rules of Online Influence

webby2011 Tom Webster
My Klout update: Currently a 59, with @Oprah at 65. C'mon, people - 7 more points and EVERYONE GETS A CAR.
15 Nov

How does one become more influential on the social web? We are certainly on the cusp of a revolution in the nature of influence that is being enabled by three concurrent technological developments:

1. The widespread global availability of free or low-cost Internet access
2. Easy-to-use social media tools that allow nearly anyone to become a publisher
3. Algorithms from companies such as Klout and PeerIndex that identify, assess, and sort influencers by topic

But apart from technology, the entire nature of influence is changing. The reason people become powerful through social media platforms such as Facebook, YouTube, and Twitter has turned many traditional ideas about influence upside down.

To understand the new realities of power and influence—and how we can use them to our advantage—it would be useful to look at some traditional views and examine what's different now. To guide us, let's turn to a well-known resource created by Dr. Robert Cialdini in his acclaimed book *Influence: The Psychology of Persuasion.*

In writing the seminal book, Professor Cialdini spent three years going undercover, applying for jobs and training at used car dealerships, fund-raising organizations, and telemarketing firms, to observe real-life situations of persuasion. The book documents what Cialdini calls the "weapons of influence" as he found them in the real world. If you want to learn how personal power and persuasion really works, this is the place to go.

Let's examine how some of these traditional aspects of influence play out on the Internet. In this chapter we'll consider authority (both real and perceived), likability, consistency, and scarcity. In Chapter 4 we'll look at two of the social web's heavyweight sources of influence: social proof and reciprocity.

At the end of each section, there are some ideas about the implications for your online power and influence.

Authority

Authority is one of the most interesting topics in considering the social web because theoretically, there isn't supposed to be any!

In fact, any attempt to impose hierarchy, rules, standards, and governance on the web will almost certainly be met with strong resistance. Wasn't the Internet built by volunteers with a mission of equal access and fairness? Isn't the Internet the great equalizer of humankind, giving a voice to anybody in any corner of the globe? Yet authority is unquestionably earned every day on social media platforms. Even the term for your Twitter connections—*followers*— implies a hierarchical structure.

Although the Internet does not have the kind of structure or organizational chart you might find in a company, a country, or even a classroom, humans crave authority and have a need to bestow authority even when it's not readily apparent. We want to know who is in charge.

Cialdini thinks this need is wired into our systems to such an extent that humans respond intuitively and even automatically to perceived authority figures. This is a very important concept as we seek to understand how people create influence, or the perception of influence, on the social web.

"Conforming to the dictates of authority figures has always had genuine practical advantages for us," Cialdini said. "Early on, authority figures—for example, parents, teachers—knew more than we did, and we found that taking their advice proved beneficial, partly because of their greater wisdom and partly because they controlled our rewards and punishments.

"As adults, the same benefits persist for the same reasons, though the authority figures now appear as employers, judges, and government leaders. Because their positions speak of superior access to information and power, it makes great sense to comply with the wishes of properly constituted authorities. It makes so much sense, in fact, that we often do so when it makes no sense at all. Once we realize that obedience to authority is mostly rewarding, it is easy to allow ourselves the convenience of automatic obedience."

In Chapter 2, we saw how this played out with people autoresponding to tweets from people they trust. This is a great illustration of the power and benefit of personal brand building on the social web. If you ascend to a position of trust on the social web, this mindless obedience is not always negative; it offers a shortcut through the density of modern life. Once we have made up our minds that a person is an authority, it allows us an appealing luxury: We don't have to think so hard about issues anymore. We don't have to sift through the blizzard of information we encounter every day to identify relevant facts; we don't have to expend the mental energy to weigh the pros and cons; we don't have to make any further tough decisions.

Instead, all we have to do when confronted with many challenges is turn to the sources we trust and play the same tape.

This concept might sound strange, but here's an example of how it works in a positive way. Marketing consultant Danny Brown spends more time tweaking and improving his blog than anybody else I know. We seem to be aligned on most business issues, our approaches to blogging and community are similar, and I trust him completely as a business professional. This relationship creates a competitive advantage for me because I don't have to hire an IT person to keep me on top of the latest blog technology innovations; I simply follow Danny's lead (and have told him so). I don't have to spend time exploring new technologies, experimenting, beta testing, and negotiating with suppliers. I just do what Danny does.

In my sphere, Danny is highly influential because he has completely earned my trust, and now when it comes to blog technology innovations, I'm in autoresponse mode. For me, it's efficient. He is my blog R&D department. Though Danny has no official authority over me on the basis of position or title, he certainly influences me and many others through authority built on helpfulness, hard work, knowledge, and integrity. There is good reason why any strategy on the social web begins with an emphasis on authenticity and honesty: It's a source of tremendous power.

Research bears this out. Base One, a London-based B2B agency, surveys procurement professionals across Europe every year to detect changes in the ways those professionals are acquiring information for their decision-making process. As you might expect, the number of people utilizing social media sources such as blogs in the purchasing profession is increasing year over year, especially among those under age 30. But here's where it gets really interesting. Bloggers are rated as the most influential sources of information. Higher than supplier websites. Higher than trade shows. Even higher than the word-of-mouth recommendation of a fellow professional.

When I first saw this statistically robust report, I was surprised, but the more I thought about it, the more it made sense. Bloggers are passionate about what they do and are usually expert witnesses to developments in the industry. Their reputations are built on their ability to provide an insider, passionate, and balanced perspective because their reputation depends on it every day.

Little wonder that a positive word from Robert Scoble made the registrations on Quora quadruple in 48 hours. The autoresponse from his readers was, "I trust Robert because he is a voice of authority."

A pundit wrote an article stating that every company needed a Robert Scoble—a high-profile voice of authority—and made his case by creating a chart with the stock value of Rackspace (his current employer) before and after it hired Robert. I'm not sure you can completely attribute a soaring stock price directly to your blogger, but the point is that a lot of value is placed these days on the trust that comes with that kind of content-based influence. If readers associate the trust and authority of a blogger with your brand, it can certainly create a halo for your company.

Although Danny Brown and Robert Scoble are good examples of authority and the new class of Citizen Influencers, one of my favorite examples of this principle is the Fiskateers, scrapbooking moms who are directly producing financial gains through the trust and influence provided by their social media presence. This wonderful marketing success was engineered by Geno Church and the Brains on Fire Agency for the Fiskars Scissors brand.

Authority in the Trenches

If Fiskars had approached me to create passion and engagement for its scissors in a way that would lead to a measurable increase in sales, I probably would have passed. Sure, it's a great product, but is there anything more mundane than scissors? Yet the agency succeeded through a brilliant integrated marketing program that leveraged the authority of Citizen Influencers.

After about a year of research, Fiskars decided there was an opportunity to create community around a group of people who were passionate about scrapbooking and the tools they used in their hobby. Through the agency, Fiskars identified four lead Fiskateers, a name the women came up with themselves, who became the brand's spokespersons on a company blog. In essence, the company turned the voice of the brand over to its most passionate customers.

Think about the validation that comes from the stories of the Fiskateers versus the press-release pabulum you see on most company blogs. Customers become influential advocates when they are able to connect their passion to a product and shape its message into their own.

The original goal was to start with four Fiskateer customer-bloggers and perhaps have 50 more brand advocates come on board throughout the country. Today, there are more than 8,000 Fiskateers, but most important, turning the brand over to these new Citizen Influencers showed measurable results:

- Online conversations mentioning Fiskars by name increased by 600 percent.
- Eighty thousand positive comments about the company were generated.
- Stores that were visited by a lead Fiskateer experienced a 300 percent increase in daily sales.
- The Fiskateer community generated ideas for several new product launches.
- The company estimates that it receives a 500 percent annual return on the amount it invests in the Fiskateers community.

The success of this program relied on the ability of the company to identify and nurture brand advocates. In this case, people from Fiskars actually walked the halls of conferences and conventions seeking these powerful word-of-mouth influencers. They found that there are people out there—thousands of them—who are passionate about their scissors. Those Citizen Influencers became marketing gold. Scrapbooking mommy bloggers ignited an epidemic of scissor love. (I guess you could say they were on the cutting edge.)

Today, there are easier ways to find and ignite people who are passionate and influential about your product, brand, and company. As we'll see in the following chapters, that's where companies like Klout and PeerIndex come in.

Perceived Authority

In these examples, the bloggers and brand advocates established their authority through their expertise and passion. Sometimes, however, even the flimsiest perception of authority is enough to get people to act. In his book, Cialdini cites a famous and disturbing example that illustrates this concept.

A group of researchers became increasingly concerned about the extent of mechanical obedience to doctors' orders on the part of nurses. Even highly trained and skilled nurses were not using critical thinking to check on a doctor's judgment; instead, they would simply defer to the physician's directives (autoresponse).

One of the researchers made a call to a hospital in which he identified himself as a hospital physician and directed the answering nurse to give a large dose of a drug to a specific patient. There were four strong reasons for a nurse's caution in response to this order: (1) The prescription was transmitted by phone, in direct violation of hospital policy. (2) The medication was unauthorized; the prescribed drug had not been cleared for use. (3) The prescribed dose was obviously and dangerously excessive. The medication containers clearly stated that the maximum daily dose was half of what had been ordered. (4) The directive was given by a man the nurse had never met, seen, or even talked with on the phone before.

In 95 percent of the instances, the nurses went directly to the ward medicine cabinet, secured the ordered drug dose, and started for the patient's room to administer it. It was at this point that they were stopped by a secret observer, who revealed the nature of the experiment.

Bloggers may not have the societal authority of a physician and don't wear symbols of authority such as lab coats or police uniforms, yet there are certainly many badges and symbols on the Internet that can reliably trigger our compliance in the absence of the genuine substance of authority. This faux authority will be covered in depth as we examine social proof.

Implications for Your Personal Power and Influence

Although some people may assume that the Internet is leaderless and rudderless, that is not the case. Many of the real and perceived trappings of authority exist in the online world. The implication of new media platforms is that anybody can become a Citizen Influencer, from a passionate scrapbooker to a dedicated blogger.

We've also seen how many people, overwhelmed by information and the density of modern life, are conditioned to look for decision-making shortcuts ascribed to real or perceived indicators of authority. This fundamental psychological principle can lead to an autoresponse, and without extreme care and due diligence, that can be dangerous.

Right or wrong, the implication is that well-known online badges of status such as the number of Twitter followers or a Klout score may be associated with authority, just as people wearing lab coats may be seen as authoritative even though they are not actually doctors.

However, as we will see, the scarcity of true authority is a powerful commodity with more lasting impact than the short-term perceived authority of social badges. Nurturing these numerical badges alone will probably not produce long-term influence on the web unless some substance, usually in the form of meaningful content and a large engaged network, is there to back it up.

Consistency and Commitment

People mistrust those who waffle. A person whose beliefs, words, and deeds don't match may be seen as indecisive, confused, or two-faced. On the other side, a high degree of consistency is normally associated with intellectual strength, logic, rationality, and honesty.

Think of the powerful implications of this perception in the context of the social web. In our carbon forms we may keep our views to ourselves or share them with close friends and family members, but on the Internet we are publishers. Our comments are permanent and searchable. There is no escape from our historical thoughts and opinions.

Blog posts and comments on blog posts may last as long as there is electricity running through servers somewhere. The U.S. Library of Congress said it is storing every public tweet as a chronicle of our life and culture. That rip-roaring-drunk tweet or the "just broke up with my cheating boyfriend" status update may have just entered the historical record. The excuses of "I was misunderstood/was misquoted/wasn't there" that have served our needs for congruity so well for centuries may no longer stand up now that our opinions, thoughts, and actions are documented and easily retrieved on Facebook, YouTube, and other social networks.

But practically speaking, the speed and volume of content on the social web generally keeps most opinions buried, perhaps negating the traditional importance of consistency. "I'm not sure that a lot of the prolific content creators are necessarily slaves to consistency," said Tom Webster of the market and media research company Edison Research. "That assumes people either remember or care enough to go back to your previously held positions to spot inconsistencies. I'm just not convinced that enough people pay attention to what I've said in the past for me to worry about today's lightly held conviction."

Jason Falls, founder of Social Media Explorer, agrees: "If human beings were not able to learn, grow, and change their minds as the result of acquired learning, experience, and knowledge, most of us would still be slaves of some sort. Over time, if we don't change our minds on a few ideas, it just goes to show that the innovators of today will be the dinosaurs of tomorrow."

"The challenge with the aspect of consistency is that it shows how my thinking evolves," said noted blogger and Twist Image agency president Mitch Joel. "Maybe that's not a 'challenge' so much as an amazing opportunity, a gift. The true value in those who are consistent online is not about if their thinking sticks in the same lanes but how they evolve that thinking after the input of others (and the discourse that ensues).

"Consistency is not so much about sticking to the same train of thought as much as it is about constantly putting your critical thinking out there for the world to discuss and debate. When I write an article for the newspaper, I prefer it to have a beginning, a middle, and an end. When I write a blog post, I know—full well—that some of the ideas are half-baked and that someone else will cook 'em. To me the value is in publishing consistently because it helps with my critical thinking, and everything that comes after that helps formulate my opinions."

A more nuanced point, Tom Webster contends, is that in many subtle ways, netizens of the social web are constantly being asked to take sides on issues: "What I would suggest is that while taking stances in social media might have some impact upon one's propensity to change one's mind, the real interesting phenomenon is the drive to 'score' the web on a binary scale. The social web is eliminating shades of gray in that sense. We are, after all, continually encouraged to give everything a thumbs-up, a 'like,' or a +1. Was it retweeted or not retweeted? Yes or no."

"Well, maybe I don't want to give something a +1," he said. "Maybe I'd like to give it a +0.35. In that sense, it isn't so much about the consistency or the lack thereof of a given source opinion, or content, it's the rush to score those opinions or that content in overly simplistic terms. And it may be that people in general do perceive a need to be consistent scorers, given that their scoring is so public."

An interesting implication of this constant grading is that online influencers may be more likely to act like politicians getting votes than like thought leaders taking a stand to propel a dissenting point of view, especially when all those likes, +1s, and tweets contribute to higher indications of your influence on platforms such as Klout.

Implications for Your Personal Power and Influence

The principle of consistency and commitment in the online world closely parallels the implications it has in the offline world, with two nuances.

First, positions taken on the web are written, searchable, and probably permanent. This may make the principle even more powerful because your views have been made known in a very public way.

Second, because of the sheer volume of web information, positions in the form of mere status updates or tweets may be fleeting and evaporate soon after they are issued. The impact may be far less than that of, say, articulating a position at a press conference or board meeting.

Authenticity is prized on the social web. Be real, be honest, but be careful. Everything you say and everything you don't say reflect on your personal brand.

I once received this valuable piece of advice from an executive at General Electric Corporation: "Remember that no matter how casual the conversation, it's still a conversation about your company."

Likability

I have this great friend who was probably the best salesperson I ever knew. We'll call him Aaron . . . because that was his name.

Aaron was a former college athlete who looked like he could still sprint right onto the basketball court, even in his forties. He was well over six feet tall and supremely good-looking, with piercing green eyes, a full head of graying blond hair, and a constant winning smile. He had the coolest clothes, the most beautiful girlfriends, the best stories, and the funniest jokes. He seemed to know a little bit of something about everything and could always make a conversation more interesting. All the guys wanted to be Aaron. All the girls wanted to marry him.

In meetings, he never said much. He studiously took notes in his ever-present black leather notebook and tended to go along with the predominant sentiments. Aaron was never one to rock the boat. The ultimate team player, you might say.

But where he shined was in his role as a sales account manager. He had this uncanny sensibility for building relationships with even the most obstinate and disagreeable customer. His Rolodex file (like many salespeople, he hated technology) was bursting at the seams with details on all his customers, their families, their hobbies, and their quirks. He drove our administrative assistant crazy sending out cards. Birthdays. Anniversaries. Thank you notes. Any excuse to connect and keep in touch. And he really meant it. This guy thoroughly loved people, and his hundreds of friends loved him back.

His customers treated him like family. He was invited to their weddings and personal celebrations. Aaron even went on vacations with his customers: skiing, hunting trips, sailing in the most glamorous locations. He was just so much fun to be around. Parties were livelier, conversations more interesting, jokes much funnier.

His influence on his customers and our business was mesmerizing. There was no problem or complaint he couldn't handle. He was our closer. Any mess we were in with customers, we could hand Aaron a plane ticket, and it would all be okay in a couple of days.

Many years later, I was in a position to hire my old friend for a marketing position in the company. It was a risk. He was so good at sales that we were hesitant to move him in another direction, but we realized he deserved a shot at this promotion.

As I went through a process to evaluate candidates, I took his longtime boss out to lunch to discuss the situation. "This may sound like a stupid question," I said as I sipped my iced tea, "but this is going to be a marketing position that will require a lot of analytical skills and technical knowledge. Is Aaron smart?"

Aaron's boss thought for a moment. Then another moment. And finally he said rather sheepishly, "I really don't know."

I think we were both a little shocked to realize that we had worked with our colleague for 10 years and couldn't accurately assess his ability to learn the skills needed for the new job. In fact, neither of us could name one of his original ideas or contributions that extended beyond the customer relationship. Yet he was incredibly good at what he did. It dawned on me that Aaron's tremendous power and influence extended completely from his likability.

There are probably situations in your career in which you've observed somebody mysteriously climbing the company ladder based less on capability than on the ability to schmooze with the right people at the top. On any organizational chart, it's not that unusual to see examples in which likability trumps experience and expertise. (As a side note, we gave Aaron the job. It was a disaster. When he was placed in a position that was less dependent on the force of his personality, he was miserable.)

Various research studies demonstrate five components that can power influence based on likability:

- Physical attractiveness
- Similarity
- Compliments
- Familiarity through repeated exposure
- Conditioning (I associate you with something positive from repeated experiences)

In the offline world, likability is powerful and ubiquitous in nearly every personal interaction. We instantly make judgments about the friendliness of the bank teller, the new teacher, the police officer who just pulled us over for speeding. But does that likability or lack thereof translate to the online world?

Gini Dietrich is certainly a role model when it comes to establishing online influence on the basis of having a likable personality. Don't get me wrong; she also has the extraordinary capabilities that enabled her to build and run her Chicago-based PR and marketing agency Arment Dietrich effectively, but it's her charm that has won the hearts of her many loyal fans and followers.

Gini spends several hours each day creating videos, Facebook updates, tweets, and blog posts discussing her dog (Jack Bauer), her bicycling expeditions, and the number of shoes in her closet amid discussions of serious business topics. It's not unusual for her to post videos on the front page of her company's website from her hotel room, a park, or even her bike. She memorably posted a video from her family Thanksgiving dinner. Gini discusses food, friends, and frustrations. Successes, failures, and disappointments. We know when she is sad, confused, or laughing out loud. Gini is a chief executive who lets people into her life in an intimate and extraordinary way.

"I don't think it's that different whether we are online or offline," she told me. "We are attracted to people we like. So online we are attracted to the way someone writes, to the way they think, even to some of the interests and hobbies if they are similar to yours. Human beings are by nature self-centered, so often we are attracted to people who are more like us, so it's meeting a selfish need.

"For me, it took some getting used to—relating to people in a very personal way on the social web. When I started out, I was pretty buttoned up. Very proper, very corporate. Full makeup, every hair in place. But over time I became more relaxed and received very positive feedback from both friends and clients when I was just myself, wherever that might be, so I just decided to address people as if they were my friends, in whatever content I was creating

"People do want to know the people they're interacting with. Even people we would normally put on a pedestal—a traditional celebrity or influencer—we want to feel like we really know them. We want to know if they like coffee or orange juice in the morning. We enjoy getting glimpses of the inner life. For me, video blogging is one more step toward that transparency that creates a bond with the people who consume our content."

Her openness has resulted in concrete business benefits, too. "It's funny about the videos," she said. "People walk up to me at conferences or when I speak and say, 'I love your videos!' I think they feel like they're sitting in my office just chatting with me. I was at brunch a couple of weekends ago, and this cute girl came up and asked if I was Gini. When I said yes, she screamed with another 'I love your videos!' My husband rolled his eyes. The thing I like about this kind of content is that you either love me or hate me. And if you hate me, you save both you and me a lot of hassle because you already know you don't want to work with us. It's a fantastic qualifier for new clients."

Creating these intimate bonds through the Internet may seem counterintuitive to a natural networker in the offline world. After all, there are no physical cues, no body language, no subtle hints that likable people would use from their normal bag of tricks to influence others. But there is a much more powerful networking tool at work in the online world: access to information.

"If you are that gregarious, friendly networking person offline, you are usually good at it because you are able to read people and adjust accordingly," said Tom Webster. "But in the online world, there is now a lot of information about me—years of my being on the web. A smart person trying to influence me would do their research before ever approaching me.

"Think of the advantage. Compared to a cold call meeting or an interaction at a business networking meeting, you can essentially prepopulate the business relationship. Sure, you don't have body language or other visual cues, but you have so much data to be able to interact about ideas and figure out what makes a person tick. If you're trying to connect with me and influence me and you haven't tried to figure me out by going back and reading three blog posts and a week of tweets, you're probably not very good at your job."

There is another factor that can distort the traditional likability factor in the online world: volume of opportunity. In Aaron's case, for likability to be a weapon of influence, there was little room for error. He had to be "on" with a small but important group of people critical to his success: his colleagues, managers, and customers. Just one detractor could jeopardize his base of power.

In the online world, however, the opportunity to connect is so vast that there may be more room for error, perhaps more tolerance for unlikability. Jason Falls explained it this way: "The Internet is not a zero-sum game. I don't have to have everybody like me or everybody think that my blog is awesome to be successful. Success for me means having enough people like my work so that I can at least provide for my wife and children in a comfortable way. And on the web, there is still enough critical mass where I can do that by being myself. I don't have to be all things to all people like you might have to consider in a corporation. Online, some people will love me, some people will like me, and then there will be some haters. In fact, when you get down to it, all I need is the marketing managers at six companies at any given time to think I am awesome to make a living. As an author, I need about 10,000 people to think I'm cool enough to plop down $25 for my book. As a person running an online community that is populated by subscribers, I only need about 1,000 people to buy into what I do out of millions on the Internet.

"The web gives people more room to be themselves and still carry influence in a niche. At the end of the day, I think those people who are really able to accomplish something and influence me are the ones who stand for something, believe in something, and will draw the line in the sand and separate themselves based on those beliefs."

Implications for Your Personal Power and Influence

Just as in the real world, likability can be a legitimate source of influence, but there are two major differences. Although we may not have the benefit of assessing somebody's looks, height, or personal style, personality is important, and the social web has the added advantage of plentiful amounts of personal information to fill in gaps and create opportunities for connection.

There is also a liberating value in honesty and authenticity, however. More people may find you influential if your personal contributions are honest. The web is big enough that you can probably find your own niche of influence even if some people disagree with you.

Likability can't be faked, but if your likability is a natural advantage for you, it is probably amplified on the social web.

Scarcity

If an item is rare, banned, discontinued, sold out, or unavailable, we seem to want it more. This principle plays out in our daily lives in many ways but was best illustrated to me as a teenager when I learned "Robert's hook."

My best friend was a guy named Robert, and we worked summers together at a famous American amusement park called Cedar Point, also known as the roller coaster capital of the world. The park is unique in that is situated a day's drive from a huge portion of the nation's Midwestern population but a short drive from nowhere. That made it difficult to hire enough students to staff the enormous park for the summer, so the company recruited clean-cut and ambitious youths from colleges around the country and housed them in dorms on the grounds of the park.

Robert and I were weight guessers. That's right. I was a midway carney, guessing weights, ages, and birth dates for a buck. It was actually a lot of fun, and I learned some great lessons in sales and persuasion. During the long, hot summer days, Robert and I worked very hard as we aimed to save enough money for the coming college semesters. But during the nights after closing time . . . well, what would you do if you were 19 years old and living at an amusement park with 1,500 clean-cut college-age women?

I was pretty naive about women and relationships, but Bob seemed to know it all. I took my cues from him, and one of his most famous moves was the hook. "If you really want a girl to like you," he said, "you need to give them the hook. You need to reject them just a little bit. Make them think you're interested in some other girl for a day or two. If you do that, they'll like you more than ever. It works every time."

And it did. At least for Robert, whose dashing good looks seemed to earn him a lot more opportunities to try the hook than I ever got. He had learned the principle of scarcity: If we can't have what we want, we want it even more.

"The idea of potential loss plays a large role in human decision making," wrote Dr. Cialdini in *Influence*. "In fact, people seem to be more motivated by the thought of losing something than by the thought of gaining something of equal value. For instance, homeowners told how much money they could lose from inadequate insulation are more likely to insulate their homes than those told how much money they could save." It may seem that scarcity is the least likely candidate to be a source of influence on the Internet. In fact, you could successfully argue that the Internet destroys the principle of scarcity. Look at what has happened to the music industry, the publishing industry, and other businesses in which "free" has become an expectation. In many cases, the Internet has disintermediated scarcity as a business model, let alone a source of influence.

Information is abundant, and almost any content can easily be found for free. For any person or company trying to monetize scarce or premium content on the social web, it seems like there is always somebody else out there willing to provide the same webinar, video, or e-book for nothing, essentially destroying the idea of a scarce resource. Chris Anderson's book *Free: The Future of a Radical Price* codifies this idea by basically saying "get used to it": You have to find adjacencies and other revenue streams because people expect Internet-based content and services to be free.

Is there anything scarce on the Internet that can serve as a source of power?

Yes, there is, according to author and college educator Christopher S. Penn. "The scarcity weapon is actually more powerful than ever on the social web," he said. "Though content may be free, what has become extremely scarce is time, attention, and influence. These are hot commodities, rare commodities.

"As an example, I have nearly 40,000 followers on Twitter. I can't tell you the number of direct messages and tweets, Facebook messages, and e-mails I receive every day asking, 'Hey, can you promote my whatever' because they know that it means something. It creates some true value.

"Attention is a resource that is scarce. True authority is a resource that is scarce. Everybody is seeking awareness and social proof, so if you are in an authentic position to provide validation, you have powerful influence.

"Scarcity plays out on the social web through the curators, the gatekeepers, the A-list bloggers: the people who have accrued the precious resource that everybody wants—the attention of an audience they can make available to you or they can keep from you. So in that regard, scarcity is a weapon that is in play like never before.

"Content on the web is like leaves that fall off trees: There is certainly no shortage. And yet if you are looking for a very special type of leaf grown in a certain climate to be used for an important medicine, then you would certainly be willing to pay an authority who can help you find it."

Implications for Your Personal Power and Influence

The Internet reframes the idea of scarcity as a weapon of influence. Leveraging or monetizing digital content can be difficult except in the rare cases in which true (and scarce) authority or high celebrity value is attached to the content.

Here's an example. Chris Brogan, the influential blogger and new media consultant, started a subscription service to provide ideas for blog posts every month. If you do a Google search for "blog post ideas" or even "what should I write about," there are hundreds, maybe thousands, of free resources out there—abundant, nearly limitless content—to help you get over your writer's block. If you or I tried to monetize such a service, people would probably scoff, and rightly so, because there is so much help already out there.

However, because Brogan has earned celebrity status among his loyal followers, his time and attention *is* the scarce commodity. An inexpensive newsletter subscription seems like a bargain to many people.

This mistake is one of the most common ones entrepreneurs make on the Internet—assuming that their content, software, e-book, game, app, or whatever is going to influence a purchase decision because of its "cool" factor. In fact, almost any digital property can be easily and rapidly mimicked unless you are protected by intellectual property rights or have the deep resources to scale so quickly and so massively that others can't possibly follow. In either case, you need deep pockets.

Most of us don't have that kind of firepower at our disposal. Therefore, our options are to either do the hard work necessary to establish ourselves as true, authoritative influencers with a loyal following—a truly scarce commodity—or partner with those who are already in that position.

The Era of the Citizen Influencer

As we have already seen in previous chapters, this is the era of the Citizen Influencer. Everybody has the opportunity to create a niche and establish a voice in his or her marketplace. Later in the book we'll look at specific ways to accomplish that.

We've taken an exhilarating little jaunt through some of the tangled relationships between influence in the offline world and influence in the online world. But we're not through.

We have two more critical factors to consider, the heavyweights of social influence: social proof and reciprocity.

CHAPTER 4

Social Proof and Reciprocity

ChristinaGace Christina Gace
Dear @Klout: You are my new favorite toy and obsession.
18 Nov

There are two weapons of influence that merit special attention when it comes to power on the social web. In fact, many people who master the concepts of social proof and reciprocity in the online world appear to be powerful even in the absence of professional experience, intelligence, or accomplishment.

Social Proof

My wife and I recently completed a lengthy mountain biking adventure. At the end of the trail, there was a quaint yellow cottage offering sandwiches, ice cream, and drinks. The yard in front of the establishment was brimming with bikes, so we figured it must be a popular place with good food. It was so popular, in fact, that the wait was too long for a snack and we rode away without ordering anything.

Hidden farther down the trail was another bistro. We almost passed it by because there were not many bikes parked outside, but we were hungry and decided to try it. We were glad we did, as we had a delicious gourmet sandwich served by a really funny waitress.

The moral of this story is that we were attracted to the first restaurant because it was validated by all the patrons it had. We nearly passed over the second place even though it had better "content" because it seemed, well, lonely.

This analogy is appropriate for the concept of social proof, a situation in which people assume that the actions of others reflect the correct behavior for them too. Just like the "votes" of bikes parked outside the restaurant, behavior is driven by the assumption that people in the same situation may possess more knowledge about what is correct, popular, or ideal—a herd mentality. As we have seen, people overwhelmed by choices may look to trusted authority figures on the web to make quick decisions, especially if those decisions are low risk. Social proof is another type of conformity.

Offline or online, when people are in a situation in which they are unsure of the correct way to behave, they often look to others for cues to the correct behavior. Social proof often leads not just to influence in the form of compliance but also to internalized acceptance as the belief that so many others *must* be correct becomes stronger.

In the offline world, people don't walk around with their number of Facebook likes plastered on their foreheads, but in the universe of the web, numerical proxies for authority abound like fleas on a shaggy mutt.

"In the world of social media, social proof is what makes you legitimate," said Jay Baer, a social media marketing consultant, a blogger, and the coauthor of *The Now Revolution*. "There are small cues on the web that convey this type of authority. There's a very good reason bloggers keep a tweet counter open at the top of their sites. If a post has been tweeted 100 times, the assumption is that it's worthy of your attention. Well, truthfully, maybe it is, maybe it isn't. There are different ways to game the online system and still be recognized as an authority. It's much easier to create a scenario and be seen as an authority online than it is to become a truly authoritative person offline."

Think of creating an authoritative scenario as the Marcus Welby effect. Robert Young was an accomplished radio, film, and television actor who represented the iconic all-American father in the 1950s TV series *Father Knows Best*. In the 1970s he reprised that squeaky-clean good-guy role for an even more famous character: the gentle, good-natured, and trusted protagonist of *Marcus Welby, M.D.* In fact, he became so tied to this character that it was impossible not to think of him as Marcus Welby in any subsequent role or appearance.

Despite his trademark portrayal of these happy, well-adjusted characters, Robert Young's reality could not have been more different. He was often described as a bitter man. He was known to suffer from depression and alcoholism, and he spoke openly about a suicide attempt in the early 1990s. Yet during that period, Young was among America's most popular television commercial spokespersons, utterly in contrast to his tormented personal reality.

Brands were able to capitalize on his social proof as a TV doctor and extend all those powerful positive attributes to their products even though the man wrapped in the white lab coat was suffering as a human being offscreen.

There has been no time in history in which the appearance of authority can be so easily assumed and promoted. Words like *best-selling, award-winning*, and *expert* have been rendered almost meaningless. We have already seen how people crave any possible shortcut to distill meaning from our information-overloaded world. Unfortunately, in this hyper environment, the badges of influence may become even more important than legitimate authority built from true knowledge and experience.

"How much do you think we'd be talking about Twitter followers or Facebook likes if the number wasn't attached to your public profile like a goiter?" asked Jay Baer in his *Convince and Convert* blog. "We care about Twitter followers and Facebook likes disproportionately not because of the power of the medium but because we keep score in public. Every legitimate social media consultant will tell you that it's not about how many Twitter followers or Facebook likes you have, it's what you do with them. And in terms of driving measurable behavior, conversions, revenue, loyalty, and advocacy, they are of course correct. Number of Twitter followers doesn't mean a thing, right? Wrong. The reality is that social media measurement is a very public competition, and we buy it hook, line, and sinker. Why would [politicians] not only [allegedly] pay to build a following that dwarfs the other candidates but then have the audacity/stupidity to brag about the advantage? Because it matters in the court of public perception."

"We may not like it," Baer continued. "We may not even choose to admit it. But it's disingenuous to suggest that number of Twitter followers has no impact on how you or your organizations are viewed by the vox populi. It's not a key performance indicator; it's a key popularity indicator."

Jessica Turner is one of America's most popular mommy bloggers at *The Mom Creative*. She has seen the power of social proof in action after five years on the social media scene: "One way to define influence *is* by the numbers—page views, followers, number of likes, etc. More important, though, is the depth of community and response. How many comments? How many e-mails of lives impacted? How many clicks? How many purchases through a link? I believe and hope the actions of the readers also demonstrate the power of a blogger's influence."

The fake Twitter account or blog site with the online equivalent of a doctor's lab coat or a bunch of bikes parked outside may well accrue benefits of influence in unequal measure to the actual skills and talents of its creator. Scarcity of attention and the daily rhythms of life and work make people default to interacting with those few who matter—or at least who *appear* to matter—and reciprocate their attention. The implication is that a possible marker of authority such as a social scoring badge can have an impact on people and contribute to the perception of one's status and influence even if it's dead wrong.

Although this idea may seem outrageous, as business professionals we have to deal with what is, not what we would like it to be, and the fact that the world is full of pretenders is nothing new. It's just that these days they may have an opportunity to find innocent victims on the Internet on a much grander scale while eluding reprisal with the simple push of a computer key.

One of these powerful new badges, as we have seen, is a Klout score, a numerical approximation of influence. Can a Klout score become a self-fulfilling prophecy? Will people seeking reassuring information from authority use these simple numerical indicators as a social badge of accomplishment? An impression of being influential can be created by, well, creating an impression of being influential.

"There is always a way to game an algorithm once you understand the data points it is taking into account," said Jason Falls. "A person can go out and create a fake online profile and within three to four months build their Klout score to a 50. Many people, even those with a good deal of social media experience themselves, would see a Klout score that high and automatically think, 'I can trust this person' without thinking, 'Who is this person, and what have they accomplished? What do they write about, where do they work, how long have they been around, are they credible, or did they magically appear out of thin air with a high Klout score?'

"What's to keep me from creating a blog and capturing somebody else's badge with the 65 Klout score and claiming it for my own? I'm not sure that most people click through to verify that status. If somebody has 15,000 followers on Twitter and makes a few lists, all of a sudden they are credible?"

One popular social media "celebrity" admitted to me that he built his entire career on faking social proof. He has accrued more than 100,000 followers on Twitter almost entirely by purchasing accounts and automated systems that build up Twitter followers and purge those who don't follow back. He rarely blogs, doesn't create any original content that would establish thought leadership, and has no customers (in fact, little business experience), but he has parlayed his image of Internet celebrity into a profitable international speaking career. He said that many sites and sponsors want to know if he has written a book. "I can't write well enough to create a book," he said, "but I tell them that I have a book in the works, and that's good enough for me to get the job."

Certainly without the credentials and experience to back him up, my friend's career prospects would appear to be limited, but in the narrow niche of public speaking, his social proof is a magic carpet of opportunity. Will it last? Time will tell, but without question, establishing social proof is an important consideration in a strategy to build influence on the Internet.

Implications for Your Personal Power and Influence

Social proof is an important weapon of influence in the offline world, but it is absolutely critical in an online world where we may never meet our virtual friends, followers, and connections. There are plentiful markers in the online world, and public numerical badges such as the number of Facebook friends or Twitter followers and a Klout score serve as shortcuts to more time-consuming assessments of actual experience.

It is politically correct for social media experts to tell you that numbers don't matter, but they're probably lying and would be challenged if their own markers suddenly dropped to zero. The care and nurturing of these badges is big business and an important source of *perceived* influence. In the long term, people will probably base decisions about your true influence on your opinions and content. But without question, badges are an important part of social proof and a factor in online influence in an information-dense world.

How do you legitimately stand out in an environment like that? Robert Cialdini said that in the "bloodless communication form of the Internet," you have to take extra steps to humanize your presence and gain real credibility.

As he describes it, "One of the things I advise when I'm consulting in corporate environments is to accentuate certain features that may be deemed attractive and include them in personal bios— the about us categories, and so on. We should be including hobbies and how many kids we have, whether we're hockey fans or runners, and so on, so people can register a connection that they wouldn't necessarily get online but is typical of face-to-face contacts. Why not infuse those online contacts with the type of information that humanizes them more and leads to cooperation and rapport?

"Researchers at Stanford University conducted an experiment and told participants they were going to negotiate through a problem as part of an exercise, but they were told that if no agreement could be reached, both sides would lose and neither side would receive credit for even participating in the exercise. When they had participants only negotiate via e-mail, 30 percent of the negotiations remained deadlocked and people walked away with nothing. However, in the instances where they had the participants exchange some personal information about themselves via e-mail prior to the negotiations, the deadlocks dropped to 6 percent. So the general human tendency is to respond positively when we know something about them, when we see something similar to us, when we see humanizing features of that person's persona available to us. Those things still work—even over the Internet or e-mail—but we have to do something to infuse those technologies with the same sort of information we might get in face-to-face interactions."

Although badges can be gamed, humanity cannot. Building social proof is important, but nurturing true authority through authenticity, meaningful content, and an engaged group of followers will lead to lasting influence and business benefits.

Reciprocity

One of my favorite stores is Colonel Mustards gourmet shop in the charming mountain village of Highlands, North Carolina. The shelves are stacked floor to ceiling with the most delectable treats: every kind of condiment, jelly, mustard, honey, and sauce imaginable. In front of each display is an open jar with crackers for samples. In other words, this place is heaven.

But as you chomp your way through cinnamon macadamia butter and chipotle mango salsa, a little guilt begins to sink in. You're eating this store owner's food. Therefore, you need to buy something. You *must* buy something. And so with $1.25 worth of samples in my belly, I typically walk out of the store with $50 worth of food products. What is the store's "conversion" rate? Almost 100 percent. Welcome to the powerful world of reciprocity.

Cialdini explains that the classic rule of reciprocity has so much impact because it's based not on the fact that we feel we *should* repay but on the idea that we feel *compelled* to. I should have bought $1.25 worth of goods or maybe nothing at all, but I was compelled to buy $50 worth.

"If a woman does us a favor, we should do her one in return," Cialdini said. "If a man sends us a birthday present, we should remember his birthday with a gift of our own; if a couple invites us to a party, we should be sure to invite them to one of ours. By virtue of the reciprocity rule, then, we are obligated to the future repayment of favors, gifts, invitations, and the like. So typical is it for indebtedness to accompany the receipt of such things that a term like *much obliged* has become a synonym for *thank you* not only in the English language but in others as well. The impressive aspect of the rule for reciprocation and the sense of obligation that goes with it is its pervasiveness in human culture. It is so widespread that after intensive study, sociologists such as Alvin Gouldner can report that there is no human society that does not subscribe to the rule."

For the entrepreneur Michael A. Stelzner, author of the book *Launch*, lessons of reciprocity became so powerful that they literally changed his business, his outlook, and his life. Stelzner bumped around a number of sales and marketing jobs before discovering a simple formula that helped inaugurate one of the fastest-growing and most profitable new media enterprises on the Internet: Social Media Examiner.

"Long after I had cut my teeth in sales and marketing," he wrote, "I discovered a better way to sell. I realized that if I simply did great things for other people, I didn't really need to ask for their help. If I did for others precisely what I wanted them to do for me, perhaps something might change.

"I discovered that most people find great value when others help them solve their problems and when they achieve recognition for their accomplishments.

"My thinking was all backward. *Rather than looking for people who would bend to my will, I needed to bend my will to people.*

Instead of asking, 'What have you done for me lately?' I needed to ask myself, 'What have I done for you lately?'

"This marked a paradigm shift in my thinking."

Indeed, whatever power structure exists on the social web, it is often built on a foundation of subtle indebtedness, an ability to create influence through an economy of favors.

"Much influence on the social web is built on a promised return of favors," said Tom Webster. "We coexist every day on small favors, like if you retweet this, I'll retweet yours. I'll like your page if you'll like mine. The effort to accomplish these things is low, so they are easily done."

The Fluffy Bunnies

"The expectation of reciprocity angle is definitely amplified on the social web," said Jay Baer. "There is this 'fluffy bunny, unicorn brigade' out there who see the opportunity to use a quid pro quo to improve everybody's relationships, which isn't bad, but for those of us who see it as a business, we struggle against the notion of this constant obligation of reciprocity, this implied obligation to return favors. That is actually the end of community. If you have to abide by a formula of reciprocity, you are trying to create authority that wasn't earned. It's not authority based on skill or how good you are at creating content, or how deep is your thinking; it's an authority created by shame and guilt! That is simply a false construct."

"I don't think power and influence on the web can be built in the long term with quid pro quo," he continued. "Sometimes you need to take the first step and give a gift to somebody, take a risk. Sometimes it doesn't pay off, but it might. And the chances of a business relationship resulting are much better if you don't expect, well, I did this for you, now you have to do this for me. It seems counterintuitive, and I *know* it's counterintuitive for big companies. They may think, Why would I do this if there is no assurance of return?"

"The same thing happens on my blog," he explained. "Every time I create a blog post, there are at least eight people I know who have bots set up to automatically pass my post along and thereby endorse it. They haven't read it. They will never read it and have no idea what the blog post is about, and there's a lot of that going on out there. But they do it because they expect you to respond in kind. That's not true authority, is it? That's expecting favors. Are they going to influence me? Probably not. Am I going to return that kind of favor?

Probably not. And yet, the social web is preoccupied with power based on reciprocity."

Mike Stelzner says that to him reciprocity means more than exchanging small favors. It's a business lifestyle. "Let's think about what relationships are really about," he said. "Business is personal. Strong business relationships on the web are built on trust that is selfless. If your child gave you a gift, would you expect that you would have to return a gift to them? Have you ever seen a wedding gift sponsored by Nike? Have you ever had to watch a 30-second commercial before you were able to open a gift? These things are ludicrous in a social media context. Why in the world of business do we think these things don't matter to people?

"Relationships still matter. Trust still matters. If you are a generally nice person and a company that is delivering great content on the social web, I guarantee you that those people and their friends are going to say, 'I just love this company. I love what they're doing, and they really seem to want to help me.' That is going to bring people back. That's how you get lifted up and grow. But if you just expect people to help you just because you've helped them, you've got it all wrong."

This selfless way of giving gifts of content, advice, and support has a powerful multiplier effect on the social web because the good deeds are experienced not just by the recipient but by potentially countless others who observe the act or perhaps hear about it. Selflessness creates legends. Legends wield tremendous influence.

This type of selflessness plays out every day on the Internet in powerful ways. One of my favorite stories illustrating this principle was from my friend Srivanos Rao, an entrepreneur who is a contributing columnist to my blog {grow}. Here's his story:

> When I look at social media, I don't see a way to lower your cost of marketing, increase ROI, or grow your brand. What I see is access to a global network of inspiring people.
>
> You see, the benefits of blogging, tweeting, and social media extend far beyond the walls of your business and the depths of your pockets. When you take the approach of making friends instead of followers, the world opens up to you in ways that you never imagined possible.
>
> A few weeks ago, I sold everything I owned and left the United States to move to Costa Rica with a few pairs of shorts, some T-shirts, a surfboard, a laptop, and a camera. That's it. I

think you'll see why concentrating on friends instead of follow-ers has helped my journey in immeasurable ways:

A pillow under my head: I recently had a chat with John Falchetto, one of my favorite bloggers. Perhaps it's coincidental that I found an expat life coach just in time for my relocation to Costa Rica. In my chat with John, he told me something that really struck me. He talked about the importance of connecting with people who are not your clients. I'm not one of John's cli-ents, and he's not one of mine. So you might be thinking, why connect? Because we're authentically interested in each other as people.

Shortly after I arrived in Costa Rica, I was invited to speak at a conference in New York City. I hardly had the resources to be in a place like New York City for 10 days, since I'm on a tight budget. A few days ago John offered me a pull-out couch in his room. So now I have a place to sleep. But I didn't connect with John because he had a couch for me. It was because I like his story and I think what he's up to is interesting.

A second family: Adjusting to life in another country can be a challenge. For me the whole expat experience has had its share of ups and downs, and there are days when I feel like living the dream is more like living a nightmare. Fortunately, I've had somebody like Mark Harai to help ease my transition to my new life. If you spend even a few days at his house, you'll quickly find yourself with a second family. There's never a dull moment in his household with four kids, and his wife will make sure you are well fed. How did I find my second family? It all started because of our conversations on Twitter. That's where we met. What's even more interesting is that it has actually resulted in us doing business together even though that was not our original intention.

A suit: When I found I'd be speaking at this New York con-ference, I realized I didn't have a suit. Just shorts, remember? When I wrote about this in a recent blog post, my social media friend Dino Dogan offered to send me a suit so that I wouldn't have to buy one and bring it back to Costa Rica. I don't know how or if we'll ever do business together, and neither does he. But you can be sure that when I have the opportunity to return such a favor, I'll do it with no questions asked.

Conversation for the sake of conversation: When I recently spoke with Dino, he told me one of the smartest things I've ever heard. He said the key to success on the social web is to completely eliminate self-interest.

It seems counterintuitive that in the process of trying to grow your blog or brand, you would eliminate self-interest. But based on my experience it seems to work quite well. We get so caught up in metrics, measurements, ROI, and more that we often forget about conversation for the sake of conversation. Helping for the sake of helping.

This is where trust is created, relationships are built, and friendships are formed. It's never about what you can get. It's about what you can give.

The human ability to detect insincerity is amplified on the social web. When we stop trying to "work the room," we tend to get the world handed to us on a silver platter.

You can see why I like that story! That is the true spirit of reciprocity, of building influence through selfless good deeds.

But indebtedness can also be effectively created on the social web with little or no effort and with quite a different effect. As Jay Baer noted, it can be created by just clicking a like button on Facebook or pushing a computer keyboard button to retweet a message to your friends on Twitter. In these cases, there is very little effort expended. And this type of low-impact reciprocity doesn't create an opportunity for influence. It creates an opportunity for leverage. There's a difference.

"Reciprocity is one of the core tenets of building relationships," said Jason Falls. "But there are people out there trying to pile on these little favors, and then you feel like you owe them for promoting your material, recommending your book, passing along links that help you one way or another. And then one day they ask for you to return the favor in a way that you would not organically support, like recommending something that you genuinely don't like. They're trying to leverage their power by trying to trade in on the idea that you *owe* them. That is not true influence because at some point I get resentful. It's not a good feeling in the relationship at that point."

The Bank of Social Capital

People say yes to those they owe. Influence through true reciprocity can drive long-term actions and behavioral change. Leverage, however, can be used only for short-term gain unless that bank of social capital is constantly refilled.

One of the Internet's leading purveyors of this social capital philosophy is Chris Brogan.

By any measure, Chris is among the social media power elite. Like so many in this new class of Citizen Influencer, Chris came from humble beginnings, the son of a working-class family in New England. He began blogging in 1998 and famously said it took him three years to get his first 100 readers, an audience that is now measured in the tens of thousands.

His source of influence wasn't wealth, a remarkable education, a distinguished business career, or a starring role in a Hollywood film. It came from being human and, above all, from being helpful. In fact, he has established an enviable new media empire of books, blogs, consulting, affiliate programs, training modules, and $22,000 speaking engagements from helpful content, a relentless work ethic, and simply being an amazingly nice guy.

Through his blog (consistently rated among the top five marketing blogs in the world), he preaches this philosophy of leveraging good deeds with aw-shucks humility.

"I don't have much power," he wrote. "What I have, however, is a lot of social capital. . . . The formula for influence has precious little to do with a few statistical data points and everything to do with understanding leverage."

Chris and his coauthor, Julien Smith, explore this topic extensively in their book *Trust Agents*: "Getting coffee for someone is doing something nice. But get your mother-in-law some chicken soup while she's sick and she'll tell the whole family how great you are. This is what the Web does all the time, but without any one individual doing the work. This is because all encounters in which you participate (i.e., all conversations you choose to take part in) are recorded in public (blogs, Facebook, and elsewhere) for others to see. You're leaving evidence of participation and good deeds to be seen by others who pass by, like markers on a trail through the forest.

"[It is] tricky to write about this without running the risk of sounding like leveraging your relationships is the equivalent of using people. This must not be the case if you are to establish successful relationships. Doing favors so that people owe you favors must not be the motivation behind developing these relationships. Do favors because you like someone, because it's the right thing to do, or because you like to be helpful. The result is that you accrue social capital as a side benefit of doing good, but doing good is its own reward. Is it wrong to think that what you do for someone will be (eventually) reciprocated? No. Is it wrong to expect it? You betcha. Don't operate with favor trading in mind. That shifts the relationship dynamic strongly toward the negative: People feel that you're always tallying, that you're looking for something whenever you come calling, along with several other personality traits that don't bode well for long-term relationships. Instead, just create goodwill."

Implications for Your Personal Power and Influence

Reciprocity can create both long-term influence and short-term leverage on the social web. Being authentically helpful and giving of your time and talent without an expectation of reward can have a multiplier effect as your goodwill is observed and noted by others. Combined with great content and an engaged network, it is probably the single most powerful creator of connection and influence on the web.

Although an expectation of short-term gain can be created by accumulating social capital in the form of low-impact favors, focus on selfless good deeds to build lasting relationships and influence. In the following chapters, we'll look at specific ways to accomplish that.

The Seventh Weapon

Authority, likability, consistency, scarcity, social proof, and reciprocity: All have their place in the offline world and on the Internet. But there is one more factor at the core of power of every Citizen Influencer, a capability that is essential, unique, and singularly important to every social media success.

Let's now discover the seventh weapon of influence.

CHAPTER 5

Content: The Seventh Weapon

rebelbrown Rebel Brown
CONTENT IS POWER
11 minutes ago

The traditional view of influence assumes that a small number of the members of our society possess qualities that make them exceptionally persuasive, driving trends on behalf of the majority of ordinary people. In business, society, politics, and the press, they may be called our opinion, or thought, leaders. Today, anybody can be a hub, a connector, an igniter of a personal epidemic of information, collaboration, and inspiration.

We can be the opinion leaders in our self-selected online societies. And by identifying and convincing a small number of influential individuals—perhaps even you and me—a viral campaign can reach a wide audience at a small cost.

In the physical world, a salesperson, a politician, or your spouse can exert influence without even owning a computer or a video camera. But to exert influence in the online world, you must create or aggregate content, have it consumed, and compel people to share it so that the epidemic—and your influence—moves to untold numbers of others.

There are parallels and manifestations of authority, social proof, scarcity, reciprocity, consistency, and likability in many examples of social influence, but *content* is the factor that twists and turns and encompasses those considerations like the air we breathe.

Content is the seventh weapon of influence.

In both the online world and the offline world, creating a network is critically important in establishing influence, but it is impossible to sustain influence in the online world without creating—and moving—consistent, compelling content. This concept is important to understand. It propels the underlying theme of this book, and by the end of this chapter you may be rethinking the nature of online influence altogether.

"If you look at social media strategy overall, there are actually two components," said the college educator Christopher S. Penn. "There is content strategy and network strategy. Content strategy is the stuff you create that is valuable to other people, and network strategy is what you have that lets you share it. Obviously they are interdependent. But if you create great content, you are more likely to have a successful network strategy.

"Content is crucial because the network part of the equation can be gamed. You can use various pieces of software and algorithms to build up a large network regardless of whether you know anything. That said, in the medium to longer term, if your content strategy is flawed, if you are not a true expert, you will burn through your network in a relatively short time. They will abandon you because there's nothing of value there.

"You see this happening with any new communication channel. In the beginning there are a lot of snake oil salesmen, but it doesn't take long—and I think the cycle is getting shorter and shorter—to figure out that this person's advice is good or that this person knows nothing but is just parroting other people.

"This is true for Twitter or Google+ or any new network, as it appears everybody is an expert at first. As time goes on, the networks change, and people start talking to each other, which is implicit in social networking. The good starts to come out, the real experts emerge, and the snake oil folks are discredited."

On the social web, consistently compelling content translates into power and sometimes fortune.

Chris Brogan dropped out of college and worked as an applications engineer for a telecommunications company but created a personal new media empire out of the power resulting from his pioneering blog.

Robert Scoble worked in a camera shop and a series of modest tech industry jobs before his simple, honest videos for Microsoft propelled him to fame and the influence sought by every start-up and gadget maker on the planet.

Calvin Lee, our mild-mannered graphic designer from Los Angeles, would probably be toiling in obscurity instead of copping free airline tickets and driving a new Audi if he weren't aggregating and promoting meaningful content.

This moment is a historic one. This is *our* time. We would never have arrived at this dawn of the Age of the Citizen Influencer without the seventh weapon—our content—and a place to post it for the entire world to see.

Even Kim Kardashian, a celebrity known for her beauty, television reality shows, and fashion sense, carries influence through to the online world only if she is producing content in the form of tweets and status updates. In fact, she is so good at it that she can charge a company $25,000 to mention its brand in a 140-character tweet. Now that's what I call the tweet smell of success. (I've been waiting three years to use that line.)

Although we have seen that the weapons of influence are present on the social web, content is the ammunition all those weapons depend on.

Therefore, if we could measure the effectiveness of that content—and track its movement and impact on others—we would be afforded a glimpse into the fundamental underpinnings of online influence. That's what companies such as Klout and PeerIndex are trying to do.

Content in Context

Let's take a step back for a moment. When I mention content, what exactly do I mean? Content is the currency of the social web, and today, creating it is as easy as typing text, uploading videos, and hitting the "publish" button. Everyone, nearly everywhere can be an influencer by becoming her or his own publisher. Here are some common examples of popular social media content.

Text-Oriented Content

Text-based content is the oldest form of mass communication and still among the most popular. Examples include the following:

- **Blogs:** A long-format content option. If content is power, blogging is the generator. Popular platforms such as WordPress and Tumblr have launched many people into the public spotlight and are also a viable source of monetization.

Blog posts can also incorporate other types of media such as video and images and usually run from a few hundred words to thousands of words. It is estimated that 330 million blog posts are published every year.

- **Case studies:** Customers and readers love success stories that validate strategies and tactics. The studies are typically one or two pages long and chronicle real-life events.
- **White papers:** These are typically 8- to 10-page topical reports that demonstrate thought leadership
- **E-books:** An extremely popular way to present complex information in a visually attractive way, e-books are usually 20 to 100 pages long and can be free or sold by the author. E-books can be in the form of simple PowerPoint slides or can be elaborate animated visual productions.
- **E-mail-based newsletters:** E-mail is a very powerful and flexible form of content marketing oriented toward a specific audience on a distribution list.

Videos

The advent of increasingly sophisticated and inexpensive high-definition video recorders and smartphones has put video production in the hands of almost anyone willing to give it a try. Nearly 50 hours of video are uploaded to YouTube, a free hosting platform, every minute of the day. Examples of popular video formats include

- Interviews
- Video blogs
- Conference presentations
- Humor
- Shopping experiences
- Music, drama, and art
- Customer testimonies
- How-to videos that instruct and teach

Presentation-Based Content

SlideShare is an easy-to-use platform to do what? Share slides! I often recommend it to corporate clients as a quick way to start sharing content because every company has PowerPoint slides, right? This is an often overlooked channel, but with more than 50 million monthly visitors and 90 million pageviews it now ranks as one of the top 250 websites in the world. Content publishing options include

I wanted to make money off of it, so I included an affiliate link to Amazon. And of course none of this could have happened without social media."

Like Kelly Hancock's successful couponing blog proves, content doesn't have to be original to be effective; it can be curated or aggregated. That's what Calvin Lee means when he refers to himself as a human RSS feed. He basically shares links from other sources and creates no significant content of his own other than his status updates. Likability alone probably wouldn't make him broadly influential on the social web. He combines that trait with interesting, helpful content.

Building an Engineering Business on Content

Imad Naffa, who proudly described himself as an "atypical engineer," built a power base on the social web as a master content curator.[1] Although he was a remarkable entrepreneur and intellect on many levels, pushing content through Twitter and engaging with his fans from around the world helped him grow his personal influence—and his business success.

Naffa immigrated to the United States from Jordan as a teenager to realize his dream of attending college in America. After graduating from Fresno State University, he found that jobs were tight. "I volunteered to work at a civil engineering firm for free," he said. "The price was right, so that was the start of my career!"

He eventually built his own business, Naffa International, to help architects and engineers understand complex building codes and regulations. Naffa was intensely interested in technology and integrating web applications to serve his clients. He pioneered the use of online forums to allow 24,000 professionals around the world to discover regulatory information and have their building plans reviewed by industry experts, a model he eventually monetized.

His family pet helped get him involved in social media. "At first I resisted Twitter," he said. "I thought it was for kids. But we started doing research on the best way to care for our pet African parrot, and my eyes were opened to the possibilities. I'm a child of information. I'm interested in a million different things, from global affairs to scientific developments, and there it all was, waiting for me on Twitter."

---

1. Tragically, my friend Imad died exactly one week after I interviewed him for this book. He was so excited to be included and such an inspirational proponent of social media marketing that I wanted to dedicate this chapter of the book to his family and his memory.

He began to experiment with a few tweets about his business, and even though engineers were late adopters of social media platforms, he found a small but enthusiastic audience. "I started following people in my industry—engineers, construction people, architects—and once in a while I would see a question on building codes, and I would jump in because I knew the answer. I would give them a link to be helpful so they could see where they could find the information on our forum. And I started to notice that a huge amount of traffic to the forum was coming from Twitter. I love data and statistics and started to think about how I could drive even more business this way—to optimize the social web as a tool to connect with people and help them.

"I began to realize that in this channel, knowledge is a valued commodity. This is a key to power and influence that most people don't understand, and I became very interested in this. I found that as I shared information about diverse topics—not just engineering—my followers grew and grew.

"I think diversity of content is important; people want to know a variety of different things. But I think you have to have knowledge and passion to be really good at social media. You can't just do what everybody else is doing. When the dust settles, I think the people who have good content, like my content, will come out on top. I communicate about a lot of things, but when it comes to my area of expertise—the building codes—I don't think anybody in the world can touch me on that stuff. And I love that. I love developing and sharing content.

"You establish relationships because of Twitter, and they watch you for a while to see what kind of content you provide. Are you the real thing? Are you consistent? Reliable? Do you have a story to tell? And when you kick a topic out there, you have to engage. You can't just ignore it. That's why you have to have knowledge and passion about your subject so you can go back and forth with your audience."

Naffa approached his content curation as both art and science, with a dashboard tracking the success of his more than 100 individual tweets every day. He was able to connect new web traffic, paid subscriptions, and new customers to his Twitter activity.

His unique role as a voice of engineering and a Citizen Influencer on the web has also paid off financially. A few of the benefits of his content curation and distribution include the following:

- More than 30 percent traffic increase to his paid website as well as measurable increases in paid subscriptions
- Invitations to speak in China and the Middle East

- Unique, global brand awareness that has led to new client contracts
- A cost-effective way to promote his business that allows him to compete with much larger firms

Of course, all his online influence has resulted in other benefits as well. "A couple of times I checked into a hotel and kidded with the front desk person by saying, 'Hey, look at my Klout score. I'm on social media, and I'm sure you want me to have a good experience.' So all of a sudden, I'm finding myself in the penthouse in the middle of San Francisco! I've also received invitations from a couple of car companies to come test drive their new models because they found me on Klout. I got a case of wine from Australia, out of left field, because I wrote about a wine experience and the winemaker wanted to thank me. I think proactive companies like that are ahead of the curve because they want people to talk about their products. I think it's a novel approach.

"It's good to see that businesses are finally paying attention to our voices on the social web, and like it or not, we're here to stay."

Thus, to use this new weapon of influence, the content doesn't necessarily have to be original, but it helps. And when it comes to original content, one of the most important sources is blogs. From mommy bloggers to tech writers, from gamers to sports enthusiasts, there are blogs that cover every conceivable passion and interest. In addition to providing a long-form free publishing format, blogs allow fans to comment and create community. The readers of blogs are often highly influenced by their favorite bloggers. Anyone, nearly anywhere, can set up camp and carve out a blogging niche for herself or himself.

Content and Celebrity

We create content, but in a way content is also creating us.

"Before the social web, there was always a ceiling or a velvet rope, a limit to where you could go with your influence unless you were somebody famous," said Jason Falls. "Now anybody can be heard. Social media and the Internet make it possible for every person to be published, find an audience, and become influential."

"Most of the people making an impact today would not have been heard from even a few years ago," he explained. "Today's crop of social media influencers probably could not have made it as far or garnered as much influence through traditional means. We would be frustrated authors, out-of-work journalists, people who had some sort of writing or media training in different formats. Even folks not necessarily trained as journalists or writers are finding that they can publish, and as long as they do it in a compelling way, they will build a large audience and continue to do so."

Jason Falls is a perfect example of a Citizen Influencer whose career was built from a dedication to blogging. As a young journalist, he dreamed of being a sportscaster or ESPN host someday. He eventually worked his way into sports information management at the college level when something magical occurred: He began to blog.

"I was hooked when I realized I could publish on the Internet at little to no cost and write about anything that interested me, not just sports but business and this new thing called social media," he said. "I saddled up and rode that horse as far as it could take me, and I'm still riding. Several years later, when I branched out from college athletics PR and into mainstream marketing, there was this groundswell of interest in social media marketing, and I realized this blog that I had been doing for so long—just for fun at that point—afforded me the opportunity to advise and help other bloggers because I had been doing it for so long. Now I have some measure of notoriety, the 'behind the velvet rope' phenomenon, being the keynote speaker at a conference. Maybe I qualify as a microcelebrity now. But of course it all happened because of the blog."

"Great content that is free of marketing messages serves to fuel the growth of your business," said Mike Stelzner. "If your business is a rocket ship, content is what makes it move. The more people consume your great content, the faster you'll grow. Not only can content improve your influence, it's also a reason for people to share your site with their friends and followers. It gives people a reason to keep coming back."

The web's insatiable demand for content is driving a different kind of influence, too: New business models based on delivering content to businesses big and small are trying to grab a piece of the social media and search engine optimization (SEO) action. From multimillion-dollar freelance-based websites to Third World content farms, content creation has become big business.

Entrepreneur Amie Marse is taking advantage of the opportunity. After starting ContentEqualsMoney.com from her living room in 2010, the Kentucky-based business is now adding employees and generating a six-figure income, all in less than 12 months

Customers usually come to her directly from her website or from third-party sites such as Guru.com and iFreelance.com.

"The content is generally in two categories," she said. "If it's for SEO, it's just going to be in the background for a search engine to see, so it doesn't even have to be very readable. We also do high-quality work for PR, websites, and articles. Obviously, that involves different skill sets and different levels of quality. The same thing goes with blogs. If you are some sort of black hat person with 1,000 websites about some sort of trinket, our articles will be very generic.[2] We will make them unique, but they're not going to have much meat to them. On the other hand, we also write for companies where we have to bring quality. We have to absorb the information and then generate content that brings something to the discussion—you've got to be saying something."

Changes to the way Google considers original content in its search engine rankings has been a boon to the content-generation business. An emphasis on original content—from doctors' offices to Fortune 500 companies—is likely to continue to drive the content industry far into the future.

Content and Social Proof

Content is so important and pervasive on the social web that it can create influence even in the absence of experience and true authority. On the web, it's not unusual for tremendous popularity, authority, and influence to accrue separately and apart from real expertise.

"There is often a disconnect," explained Mitch Joel, president of the Montreal-based digital agency Twist Image. "The ability to drive results for a company has little relation to your ability to create compelling content for your audience. I'm not sure that most people who consume the content or take part in the social engagement understand that just because somebody has a knack for writing or can put some great ideas together, it doesn't mean they have a knack for

---

2. The term *black hat* refers to search professionals who use questionable, unethical, or even illegal practices to win favorable product placement on search engine results.

taking those ideas to market and delivering a return on investment. So it's interesting and a bit dangerous to think that publishing and moving content is necessarily the same influence you really need to run a business."

Is that kind of influence sustainable? Can real personal influence be built on content that is unsubstantiated by personal performance, authority, intellect, or experience?

Dr. Robert Cialdini thinks it can because of the interaction between powerful social proof and content that is unique to the web: "It's true that with content, we create value because we give people access to insights they didn't have before. That's not unusual—we've always had opinion leaders of groups who have coteries of people listening to them because they provide valuable insights. What's interesting on the Internet is the social proof aspect of this. People will perceive the value of the individual and the content based on how many other people are accessing it. That's evidence of its validity.

"That's the fundamental insight that comes from the concept of social proof—the fact that people believe something because other people are thinking something or doing something and that gives the content validity. There is no greater logic associated with it, there is no greater empirical evidence associated with it; the simple fact that other people are accessing it is the social proof."

"This validation concept works at the neural level of brain activation," he continued. "When someone in an experiment finds that other individuals in that experiment have rated a face as more attractive than they did originally, not only do you get the normal conformity effect where people will now rate the face as being more attractive, when you look into their brains—using MRIs—the sections of the brain associated with value are activated by this evidence. So it's a fundamental human process to assign more legitimacy, more validity, more value, to those things that other people are assigning value to. So we get to augment the valuation of content in a way that is apart from merit through the mechanism of social proof, which the Internet provides in ways that we have never seen before.

"People who might be upset by this fact have a case to make. The Internet offers an unprecedented opportunity to manufacture social proof through tricks and devices. In the same way that it is possible to override the validity of any fundamental principle once you understand how to trick it, it's possible to market your own prominence through strategies that don't have anything to do with the real insights or value of what you provide. You structure your algorithms on Amazon to do it, or Klout to do it, and the like.

"It's reminiscent of what the historian Daniel Boorstin wrote in his classic book *The Image* when he compared his day to a time before mass media when celebrity was associated with genuine accomplishment. In fact, you could only become a celebrity based on what you had accomplished. But then he remarked on the new form of celebrity where the accomplishment was *becoming known!* The accomplishment, then, is figuring out how to become known. And we seem to have that now with Internet stars and reality TV stars who learned how to game the system. So I can see why there is some negative reaction against these influence ratings because on the one hand, they do provide something genuine and valid, but on the other hand, they can be tricked. I can understand why somebody would want to hold back our wholehearted enthusiasm for such rankings."

As we take another step toward this book's examination of the usefulness and ability to measure an individual's online influence, this brings us to a vital conclusion:

Because of the Internet's vast ability to grant social proof and our increasing willingness to accept that evidence as truth, the talent to create and distribute meaningful content can be a legitimate source of online influence even apart from an individual's actual experience, capability, or personal accomplishments.

A strange idea, isn't it? In the offline world, we expect our influencers to earn their status through performance. Surgeons had better perform successful surgery. Chefs had better make wonderful meals. Movie stars had better make movies that appeal to us. But that is not necessarily the case on the Internet. Nothing has to be real. One famous author and consultant from the website *Men with Pens* built up a loyal group of fans and a profitable base of clients, only to reveal years later that he was actually a she. Her entire persona was faked. Content was her only calling card.

Disconnecting our personal traits from the ability to influence can be dangerous, but it can also be liberating. Influence built on content—our own hard work, our own voice—can free us from the shackles of traditional trappings of influence associated with going to an Ivy League school, living in the right part of town, having movie star looks, or driving an expensive car.

Today anybody anywhere can have influence, and that is a great thing.

Implications for Your Personal Power and Influence

This chapter explores the surprising notion that meaningful, compelling, and entertaining content can significantly contribute to online personal influence even apart from experience and competence. But of course the key to success for both individuals and businesses is to create excellent content that will cut through the clutter and then move others to consume and share it virally through a network.

"We all know that the social customer is not only gaining influence but also is inundated with content," said Michael Brito, senior vice president for social business planning at Edelman Digital. "Consumers who live in the 'stream,' that is, Twitter, the Facebook news feed, FriendFeed, Google Reader, for example, are inundated daily with thousands upon thousands of marketing messages. As a result, they are filtering out the content that is not relevant to them. Everything else is noise and usually is ignored.

"From a brand perspective, the challenge is equally clear. If they want their messages to be heard, understood, and believed, they have to fight for the attention of the social customer. And they have to do this one of two ways. First, they have to be omnipresent on the social web and leverage multiple customer touch points with the same message. Omnipresent simply means that brands need to use paid media (display ads, search, out-of-home, broadcast), earned media (influencer and advocate outreach programs, events), and owned media (Twitter, Facebook, YouTube, blogs) to reach consumers with the same or similar messages. Second, their messages have to be relevant. Individuals need to hear/read/see things three to five times before they actually believe them. So every form of content has to be consistent in order to break through the clutter in a relevant and authentic manner."

This concept is growing more elusive as millions upon millions of individual posts, photos, and videos are uploaded to the Internet every minute. The ever-present challenge is to stand out. Of course, standing out is dependent on your niche and your audience, but there are some guidelines that seem universal.

RITE

In my classes, I encourage students to focus on creating content that is RITE: *r*elevant, *i*nteresting, *t*imely, and *e*ntertaining. If you consistently hold this filter up to any content you create, you'll be on your way to creating value that becomes part of the signal instead of the noise.

Relevance

"Relevant content adds value to the conversation," said Michael Brito. "And many companies today are not sure where to start. One way to determine if and where the conversation is happening about the brand is to conduct a conversation audit. A conversation audit uses social listening software platforms such as Radian6, Meltwater Buzz, or Sysomos to data mine the Internet for brand- or product-related conversations." He said that data from such an audit will give an organization insight into the following:

- Where the conversation is happening (Twitter, Facebook, forums, blogs)
- Nature of the conversation (sentiment, product, brand, or both)
- Share of voice in comparison to competitors or the general market category
- Influencers' identification; their total reach, their community size, and where they spend most of their time online
- Competitive audit: competitors' community size, growth rate, and web traffic

Individuals may not have access to these paid resources, but there are also many free and effective ways to gauge the state of the conversation for your particular audience:

- Listen before you leap. Take some time to understand a particular channel and its audience before beginning your content development.
- Subscribe to blogs, Twitter feeds, and YouTube channels that will help you get a feel for the content that is already out there.
- Set up RSS feeds, Google alerts, and Twitter searches on keywords relevant to your topic and audience. For example, in preparing to write this book, I set up a Google alert for "Klout" that allowed me to read a stream of articles and blog posts people were writing about this subject. It helped me learn about the sentiment toward Klout, identify possible case studies to include in the book, and find some interesting people to interview.

Interesting

The next aspect of RITE content is "interesting." Although this may seem obvious, creating material that is consistently compelling may be the most difficult task of all, but it may also have the biggest payoff.

"In the past, many companies relied solely on press releases to launch products," said Brito. "Others have leaked product information to tech influencer blogs in order to leverage their reach, influence, and community size and create buzz. The problem with these two methods is that they result in a one-time communication opportunity. After all the hype and buzz dies down, there is no way for a company to communicate with the social customer again."

By contrast, creating consistently interesting content provides an ongoing focal point to a company or individual. Instead of relying on the big bang theory of press release distribution, smart organizations are empowering their employees to blog and tweet to establish these connections and influence. This setup also establishes a connection directly between the company and consumers rather than relying on a third party to carry that message. Similarly, individuals are realizing that power comes from engaging an audience through interesting and authentically helpful content.

How can somebody become more interesting? After all, aren't some people naturally more interesting than others?

I believe that every person can develop compelling content. Here is the challenge I pose to anybody seeking to provide a guest post to my blog: Write something that could have been written only by you. The world doesn't need another blog post about "The Five Biggest Mistakes on Twitter," but it might be really interesting to read about "My Twitter Epiphany" or "My Personal Twitter Catastrophe."

Ultimately, our only true point of differentiation is ourselves. How does the subject relate to *you:* your observations, your experiences, your life, your stories? This isn't narcissism; it's the soul of originality. Think of the power and excitement that would be unleashed if a company leveraged the uniqueness and insights of its employees instead of pummeling us with press releases.

Better yet, why not involve the stories and passions of your customers as Fiskars did? Another great example of this is Patagonia, an outdoor gear retailer that features the adventure stories of its readers on its excellent corporate blog. Wouldn't it be more interesting to read about a hiker using his gear to survive a blizzard than to read a press release on new fiber-fill technology? Let your customers carry the flame of passion for your products.

If you look at any piece of content that goes viral on the social web, it nearly always taps into some form of honest human emotion—or cats (but that's a subject for another book, I suppose).

Compelling content doesn't have to be profound. It doesn't have to be a PhD thesis. But it does have to be human. Michelle Chmiliewski, a marketing professional and blogger working in Paris, noticed how the citizens of her adopted country seemed to use the word *putain* (French for "prostitute") in many colorful ways. She produced a clever and funny video on this simple observation that has been viewed nearly 1 million times (the web address is in the references appendix at the back of the book).

Michelle is not a professional actress. She isn't a published author or a celebrity by any normal definition of the word. She is a Citizen Influencer who created this little video while sitting in her apartment. By simply letting her personality loose on this seemingly mundane observation, she created—and moved—content in a way usually reserved for MTV stars. She had the courage to be a little goofy, a little creative, and, most of all, interesting.

Dig deep. Make it human. Be interesting.

Timely

I often joke to my marketing friends that the social media world moves in dog years. The amount of change that used to take seven years now takes one. It seems that if I'm off the grid for even a couple of weeks, the world just passes me by. Because of this rapid pace of change, content consumers place a tremendous value on information that is timely.

"This is not a new idea," said Shelly Kramer, founder of the V3 Kansas City Integrated Marketing Agency. "In any generation, people have a thirst for the latest knowledge and trends. Marketers and content creators only have an advantage if they don't become stuck in the rut of traditional ways of doing things."

"We do a lot of content creation work with our clients and often approach it from an angle of offering something exclusive, up to the minute, or behind the scenes," said Gini Dietrich. "We work with a client that does oxidizers, which are about as big as the first floor of a house. They are gigantic. You can actually walk inside one of these things, but normally you can't because of EPA regulations. The only time you could really see inside of one is when you're installing them, so we took some cameras out to record the installation of one of these pieces of equipment as they're putting it together. Right on the site. Right as it's happening. By connecting in the moment, we were in a position to show our customer as a real thought leader because they are the only ones doing this kind of 'sneak preview.' And people in the industry just loved it. If you can create content that makes people feel like they are part of something—that they are getting something exclusive—it works really well."

I like this example because it shows the power of simply thinking in terms of now. What might have been thought of as a routine installation of an industrial facility has been transformed into a rare behind-the-scenes look at a project that is probably interesting to a lot of potential customers.

Here are some ways you can emphasize timeliness in your content creation:

- Surround yourself with people and resources that will keep you abreast of the latest developments and ideas in your industry or field of interest.
- Subscribe to an RSS feed of journals and blogs covering developments in your business and check it every day. Depending on the rate of change in your business, you may need to check it several times a day.
- Emphasize speed in your content creation. Be the first to comment on a trend or an announcement.
- Connect trends and developments to real business implications. What does this mean to your customers? What does it mean to you?

Entertaining

Entertainment value is not a term commonly used in most businesses, yet with the cacophony of voices vying for your attention, isn't entertainment paramount today? Are you more likely to enjoy and remember a post titled "An Analysis of SEO Implications for Blogging" or one titled "How to Be a Google Whore" that uses humor to illustrate the dead-serious issue of the overuse of keywords in content creation? Mix it up. Add video, photos, interviews, reviews, and humor. Be surprising.

I started adding an original cartoon to my blog every Friday simply for the entertainment value. It's a unique feature that I hope helps my content cut through the clutter yet still inform and engage.

Nathan Dube, a marketing manager for a Massachusetts office supply company, inserted a little entertainment value into printer maintenance services. He was faced with a problem: create brand awareness for a product—printers and office technology maintenance contracts—that most people hate. After all, aren't printers our biggest obstacle to personal productivity? But it gets worse. He had no marketing budget.

The solution? Create a contest featuring the most creative way to destroy your printer. It was hosted, promoted, and entirely managed using free social media resources such as YouTube and Facebook; Nathan encouraged his friends and followers to submit videos of the most creative and entertaining ways to destroy a printer. He capitalized on the idea that the new technologies are enabling everyone to be a content creator.

People from around his region and eventually from around the country submitted home videos from smartphones and cameras of their useless printers being tossed from buildings, pounded by sledgehammers, obliterated by backhoes, and vaporized by dynamite. In other words, it was a lot of fun.

By tapping into a customer emotion and inserting some entertainment value, Nathan ignited an epidemic of fun that resulted in massive awareness for his products, hundreds of sales leads, and several new long-term customer relationships.

Ignition

Think of the Internet content you love the most. It may inform and enlighten, but chances are that the content you share is something that is entertaining. Of course RITE offers a simplistic shorthand version of a content strategy, but it's a good start. Chapter 9 offers more content development ideas and resources.

Now that we've explored the similarities and differences of offline and online influence, let's look at why finding these online igniters is so tantalizing—and so important—for marketers. The answer might start with Marilyn Monroe.

CHAPTER 6

Personal Influence:
The Marketer's Holy Grail

ChrisQueson Christopher Craft
If my @Klout score ever drops below 50 again, I'm going to
slap myself. No excuses. #klout
4 Apr

Since the dawn of marketing, companies have been chasing influence. However, for much of advertising's history, that elusive characteristic was strictly associated with celebrity, not with citizens.

According to Thomas Mickey, an advertising and PR industry historian, the first paid celebrity endorsers were probably the stars of P. T. Barnum's circus troupe in the nineteenth century. "Barnum would have his most popular clowns and entertainers go in advance to the next city," he said. "They would be the faces on the posters and the newspaper ads, and it was quite effective. That was the first example of using the power of a character in the media of the day to get a consumer to take action."

When motion pictures and radio were introduced at the turn of the century, technology became the enabler of a new era of celebrity and companies were desperate to have glamorous stars use their products. Celebrity endorsements became commonplace. The most popular program hosts and stars would simply mention the show's sponsor during the broadcast as a means of funding the mass media entertainment.

The comedian Bob Hope began lauding the freshness of Pepsodent toothpaste. Carnation milk became associated with the radio superstars George Burns and Gracie Allen. Companies such as Procter

& Gamble, Johnson & Johnson, and Kraft built their businesses by funneling millions of dollars into the hands of newly emerging advertising agencies, which eagerly lined up celebrity talent to promote their household products.

The most popular stars of the era, Charlie Chaplin and the baseball star Babe Ruth, endorsed everything from cigarettes to cereal. Ruth's popularity as a pitchman grew to the point where his earnings from advertising far exceeded his salary as an athlete. He was probably the first individual in history who had to hire a business manager and an accountant to keep track of all the money he was making from paid product testimonials.

The most famous example of celebrity influence occurred in 1954 when a reporter offhandedly asked Marilyn Monroe what she wore to sleep. The ever-seductive Monroe purred, "A few drops of Chanel No. 5."[1]

Her famous response, which was not sponsored by the company, created an overnight frenzy of perfume sales and a legendary example of influence marketing. That single comment established Chanel No. 5 as the fragrance you wore to sleep or to charm the special man in your life for the evening. The accidental endorsement helped create one of the top-selling perfumes in history and initiated a series of high-profile Chanel spokespersons, including the actresses Catherine Deneuve and Nicole Kidman.

In the age of mass media, advertisers quickly learned the power behind the positive influence that celebrities could bring to a persuasive message. Today, approximately 25 percent of all U.S. television commercials contain some sort of celebrity endorsement, although it might be as subtle as a voice-over. Although the world's obsession with celebrity offers a profound opportunity to create credibility for a product, it also comes with a hefty price tag and the ever-present risk of being associated with star-studded scandal.

Significant investments in star power were out of reach for most companies and did not always result in predictable results. For instance, Bill Cosby, who had previously proved quite effective for JELL-O, appeared to have little effect when he was associated with E. F. Hutton and Texas Instruments.

The high price tag and risk of celebrity endorsements naturally drove most marketers to look for more cost-effective and reliable

---

1.   Chanel No. 5 was created by Ernest Beaux. In 1921, he presented Coco Chanel with two sets of five test fragrances numbered 1 to 5 and 20 to 24. The rest is history.

alternatives for creating brand awareness. The answer was quite simple, a business truth known since the time of the earliest medieval marketplaces: Connect with those neighborhood superconnectors, those epidemic starters, and your product will start to move! The challenge was finding them.

B. T. Babbit and His Soap Clean Up

Perhaps the genesis of today's influence marketing efforts was a carefully wrapped bar of soap sold from a wagon. Although B. T. Babbitt is not exactly a household name, he deserves a special place in the history of word-of-mouth marketing. A natural-born inventor, chemist, and marketer, Babbitt was like any number of people in the industrial era, trying to elbow his way into a lucrative business by selling products based on sodium bicarbonate, the essential ingredient in baking powder and soap.

The problem was that in his day, soap didn't come with the scent of an Irish spring day, lemon freshness, or powerful antiperspirants. It was boring. Everyone, it seemed, sold undifferentiated blocks of gray or brown soap. Babbitt was smart enough to know that the key to selling more was to win the hearts and attention of his city's housewives, and he took to the streets to find out how to do that.

He discovered that packaging his soap in individual bars that were hand-wrapped with paper made it easier for housewives to purchase the soap and carry it home. From the back of a brightly colored wagon, Babbitt gave out free samples of his wrapped soaps (this initiative is the source of the popular phrase "get on the bandwagon"). The breakthrough innovation caught on, and word rapidly spread about the convenience and variety of the products he was offering. Soon lines of housewives were forming at Babbitt's stores, asking for the new personal-size bricks of soap.

Although this is certainly a lesson on the importance of listening to customers, it is also one of the first examples of a business systematically identifying and leveraging everyday influencers. Babbitt knew that the most effective way to get a housewife to buy his soap would be to convince her influential friends and family members to suggest it.

Smart companies realized that preachers, car salespersons, corner store owners, and barbers held tremendous sway over a community and were often the "patient zero" for commercial viral outbreaks.

Certain family members disproportionately influenced buying decisions: Dad controlled the home repair budget, kids heavily influenced annual vacation decisions, and Mom controlled the purse strings for just about everything else.

The First Integrated Word-of-Mouth Campaign

If you boil animal bones and connective tissue long enough, you can extract collagen, which contains a protein called gelatin. It's not a pretty picture, but add a little fruit flavoring and food coloring and it can make a versatile and tasty dessert.

The problem was that when powdered animal gelatin was introduced in 1845, homemakers didn't know what to make of it. It wasn't meat, it wasn't a vegetable, and it wobbled. Nobody would touch it.

Forty years later, the patent for the powdered gelatin invention was sold to a New York entrepreneur named Pearle B. Wait. Wait was an unusual business combination of "carpenter and maker of cough syrups." He and his wife, May, saw the potential to make the gelatinous product more palatable by adding strawberry, raspberry, orange, and lemon flavoring from the cough syrup formula to the powdered concoction. In 1897, JELL-O was born.

Now the product looked a little better and tasted much better, but the family still could not figure out how to teach housewives what to do with it. After more than a decade of frustration, the Waits sold the flavored JELL-O business to a neighbor, Orator Francis Woodward, for $450.

Increasing the sales of the strange product wasn't any easier for Woodward. At first he went the traditional route by trying to raise awareness of the product through advertising in national magazines such as the *Ladies' Home Journal*, which boldly proclaimed JELL-O to be "America's Most Famous Dessert."

Sales picked up a little, but JELL-O still foundered, and the Genesee Pure Food Company teetered. Woodward knew that he had to teach homemakers how to use the product creatively. If he could do that, he felt sure they would teach others and use their influence to create epidemics for the fruity dessert. But in 1904, how would he find those influencers?

In a bold move, Woodward paid enormous numbers of salesmen to go out into the field to conduct demonstrations, provide samples, and distribute free JELL-O cookbooks, a pioneering marketing tactic at the time. The gamble worked, and the power of word-of-mouth influencers began to take over as housewives learned to create colorful Bundt-pan-molded JELL-O creations to take to their church potlucks, birthday parties, and Friday bridge nights.

With a little positive cash flow, the company began to grow the brand, adding new flavors, a pudding variety, international marketing efforts, and celebrity endorsements from actress Ethel Barrymore, opera singer Ernestine Schumann-Heink, and radio star Jack Benny, who introduced every radio show with the signature "JELL-O everybody! This is Jack Benny!"

Woodward's aggressive approach caught on. As large companies and big brands fought for supremacy over the radio and television airwaves, another group of street-savvy entrepreneurs waged battles for the consumer pocketbook on the ground. The postwar migration to suburban communities helped enable an era of door-to-door salespersons who instinctively tapped into neighborhood influencers to sell thousands of household products ranging from vacuum cleaners to encyclopedias.

Soon the streets of many middle-class neighborhoods were flooded with product-toting sales representatives. As the competition heated up and referral-fueled door-to-door sales began to mature, marketers had to evolve again. The most innovative companies discovered a breakthrough strategy that directly leveraged the power of influence in a new way.

Lipstick, Ambition, and Pink Cadillacs

One young mom, in dire need of extra income for the monthly family budget, spent a chunk of her meager savings to attend a sales convention for a company that was selling cosmetics door to door. Without even enough money for a vending machine snack, she brought her own food, discreetly munching on peanuts while she watched other salespeople win awards and receive cash bonuses.

When she was called to the stage for a minor award, she took the opportunity to whisper into the presenter's ear, "Next year, I will be the top salesperson at this convention." Surprised, the executive looked at Mary Kay Ash and said, "Yes, I believe you will."

True to her prediction, Mary Kay stepped onto the stage the next year as the top salesperson in the company. Her secret was deceptively simple: Find the influential housewife, not a professional salesperson, to do the selling for you.

On a Friday the thirteenth in 1963, Mary Kay Ash bet her life savings of $5,000 and started a new company, Beauty by Mary Kay, with the help of her 20-year-old son. Ash's model tapped directly into the likability aspect of the influencer model by making the housewife, the PTA mom, and the card party host the hero of the sales program. Wouldn't housewives buy more from their friends than from a stranger knocking at the door?

A sales and marketing juggernaut was born that today uses an effective network of more than 1.8 million influencers to sell $2.4 billion in cosmetics every year. This successful model has been replicated over and over by Tupperware, Pampered Chef, and many other enterprising home-based entrepreneurs.

Moving forward to the 1970s and 1980s, case studies on fortunes being made through the power of citizen influence abounded. For example, Procter & Gamble pioneered this approach of manufacturing word-of-mouth buzz on a large scale by recruiting a quarter of a million teens to create buzz about new products, some as mundane as toothpaste.

3M's now ubiquitous Post-it Note owes its existence to an influencer campaign led by its administrative assistants. The now-famous story of the commercialization of the weak adhesive was jump-started when the company decided to give away samples to 3M executive assistants and the residents of Boise, Idaho. Soon chief executives were showing up at their meetings with the helpful yellow notes stuck to memos and file folders. Corporate ladder climbers, eager to please, emulate, and impress, harassed the office manager to buy more of the Post-it Notes.

The Australian winemaker Yellow Tail found gold in the highly competitive alcoholic beverages market by connecting with a neglected group of influencers: wine store merchants. Although Yellow Tail had neither the pedigree of Napa Valley and French wines nor a classic taste that appealed to connoisseurs, it did have a smart executive team that understood the power of influence marketing. In fact, nearly the entire marketing budget was dedicated to sending perks such as free gear and apparel to wine store owners.

Those mom and pop shop owners, completely ignored by other brands, liked the attention and began suggesting Yellow Tail to their customers and providing the company's products with prominent positions in their stores. Remarkably, within five years Yellow Tail went from sales of zero to 7.5 million cases, becoming America's most popular wine, an unparalleled success in the beverage industry.

Database Marketing and Influence on an Industrial Scale

In the 1990s, technology worked against traditional advertising methods, and brands once again were forced to adopt and adapt to a rapidly changing landscape. Anticommercial sentiment got a nudge as cable broadcasters such as HBO seduced customers with commercial-free programming. VCRs accelerated commercial avoidance, giving customers the ability to forward past annoying 30-second messages. Media-savvy consumers used devices such as TiVo to eliminate commercial breaks altogether, and late in the decade the most sweeping change since the advent of radio shook the foundations of media empires: the widespread adoption of the Internet.

With the increasing popularity and affordability of computers and access to vast databases, marketers began finding ways to record and sort through customer purchasing records with increasing efficiency, creating an explosion of new targeted marketing options.

Companies could now distill marketing wisdom from billions of pieces of data to find their most profitable markets, products, and customers; opportunities to upsell and cross-sell; and consumer spending habits. With that information, complex models of customer behavior were created that could identify specific individuals for sampling campaigns and special offers.

Car companies used the data to invite specific customers to VIP showings of new automobiles. Magazine publishers offered trial subscriptions to targeted high-value subscribers. Entire communities were categorized and influencers pinpointed for a constant drumbeat of product samples, direct mail, and targeted advertising.

Even the tried-and-true mechanisms of celebrity endorsement could now be statistically dissected. Complex rating systems were developed to rank celebrity appeal across dozens of personality traits and demographic categories. Q scores (by Marketing Evaluations) and E scores (by Epoll) are two of the better-known measures used to match products with both living and deceased celebrities and athletes by traits, including

- Recognition
- Key personality factors that drive appeal

- Perceived personality attributes
- Appeal by demographic characteristics such as age, gender, income, and ethnicity
- Filtering and evaluation by category and by time frame

A carefully nurtured celebrity rating and high E and Q scores could mean millions of dollars in endorsements for well-known stars and athletes.

Finding and harnessing the power of influencers no longer required the finely honed instincts of Madison Avenue gurus or powdered gelatin salesmen hitting the streets to find well-connected housewives. The business strategy shifted to statisticians, algorithms, and predictive models, important building blocks for the online marketing revolution that dawned with the new millennium.

The Social Algorithm

Algorithms—repeatable computer code used to solve complicated problems—are at the heart of much decision making in the marketing world today. Combined with ever-expanding databases of personal information collected through the social web and astonishingly fast computation speeds, these powerful snippets of code can predict the types of movies you like to watch, the soft drink you are most likely to order with your popcorn, and even whether you will like a specific movie.

At first these algorithms were used to do simple tasks such as identifying the most loyal and profitable customers. However, that all changed with the pioneering work of Bob Gerstley, considered by some to be the father of social algorithms.

Gerstley started with a simple question: Can software identify the most influential person in a network? Gerstley's research combined social networking activities, group memberships, leadership roles, published content, and other criteria into a single mathematical calculation. That algorithm, when applied to a group of people in a database, would result in a numerical ranking called the Social Networking Potential (SNP). With SNP in hand, companies could quickly zero in on the VIPs in their databases. Mobile phone providers were the first to apply Gerstley's work, since they had a massive trove of data culled from phone call records.

The ability to dissect and assess billions of pieces of data instantaneously and cost-effectively to find online influencers is a natural progression of a system that had its roots in the earliest marketplaces in the world, celebrity endorsements, the JELL-O viral approach to marketing, and Mary Kay Ash. It seems inevitable, doesn't it—Q scores and E scores for every person on the planet!

Azeem Azhar, the founder of London's PeerIndex social scoring system, was a pioneer of this concept of distilling massive amounts of data into usable characterizations of everyday influence. Azhar, who describes himself as "a geek at heart," had already established a reputation as a respected British technology journalist when he began to dabble in start-ups.

"As far back as the early 2000s, I was thinking about this idea of measuring online influence," he said. "At the time I ran a blogging platform, and I was always wondering about how we could turn it into a more powerful media platform by harnessing the influence or impact of the people who were writing their posts," he said. "We were heading in the right direction with that idea, but we were a little ahead of our time in terms of the capability of technology.

"The kindling for PeerIndex began to burn during the financial crisis. Around 2008 I realized that I was getting an increasing amount of my news from Twitter, maybe even more than from the *Financial Times* or *Wall Street Journal*. It was happening because I was connecting to smart people I trusted, people who were curating content that was very relevant to me.

"So we sat around our office, thinking about all the intelligence out there! We thought that we should find a way to discover these experts and elevate those experts without having to go through the old channels."

Algorithms Elevate the Citizen Influencer

"The old channels of creating influence were quite clear . . . and dysfunctional," Azhar said. "In order to have impact, you needed to go to the right university . . . check that box . . . get a job with the right newspaper or investment bank . . . check that box . . . and guess what? Now you have influence.

"But actually, it's not influence; it's hurdle jumping. You're jumping the hurdles of your SAT, your GRE or GMAT, or other entrance exams. You're jumping the hurdle of the late-night drink with the city editor of the local paper or investment banker who you're hoping is going to recruit you. That was the old way to get ahead and get noticed.

"But we found some really smart people hanging around in this social space with no clear metric to distinguish who you should trust and on what subject. So that's what PeerIndex became. That was the vision.

"We knew that within the data on the social web there were some really clear indications of people's tendencies and behaviors," he continued. "There were patterns that would indicate the topics that they really cared about and maybe even some indicators of influence on certain topics.

"A powerful analogy for this is the personal credit rating. In that case, a corporate entity looks at all of the previous activity for a person going back 5 or 10 years and sums it up in a single number. A smart loan officer will dig through the details to make the best assessment, but if you need a quick decision, that single number will probably work.

"We realized when developing the PeerIndex application that it's kind of meaningless to say someone is a 48 without knowing what it means. You could be a 48 on average but 76 in the field of education, which means you are trusted, respected, and care about education more than most other people. But that same person could also be a 22 on the topic of baseball, which means he's kind of a hobbyist. So if you break it down like that, the numbers begin to have real meaning."

The implication of this development is that if a company wants to identify influencers relevant to its brands and products easily, a list can be assembled that it knows with some confidence will represent passionate, knowledgeable, and maybe even respected influencers at nearly every level of society.

"The *idea* of using influence in business has come a long way, but we are just at the beginning of understanding and measuring this *science* of influence," Azhar explained.

Becoming a Person of Influence

This chapter has traced marketing's evolution through media and technology, from circus posters to social algorithms. Once again, the next step in marketing's evolution is being defined by a technological advance: the free tools that allow everyone to publish and distribute content through the Internet and the formulas that measure it.

I'm living proof of that technological step forward.

I recently received an invitation to speak at a prestigious government conference and influence 700 people in real life because of one popular blog post I had written.

Another blog post I wrote showed up in the search results of a *New York Times* reporter who was researching a social media topic: social scoring. She interviewed me, and the article appeared in the Sunday edition of my favorite newspaper. The article—with my name in it—was picked up by newspapers around the world, including the *Daily Mail* in London.

Consulting work for the British government, my teaching position at Rutgers University, and even the opportunity to write this book came through connections in my social media network inspired by my content.

None of this could have happened 10 years ago. Without the social web reaching critical mass, I'd probably be toiling in obscurity in a cubicle somewhere. This is my time to be a person of influence. This is *your* time to be a person of influence. And corporate America can't wait to find you and reward you, just as it did with Bob Hope and Marilyn Monroe and Bill Cosby. Well, sort of. To understand the new world of citizen influence, it would make a lot of sense to learn a little about the company at the middle of all this, Klout, so let's do that.

PART 2

Klout and the Social Scoring Revolution

S o far we have assembled seven fundamental conclusions in our quest to understand the unique characteristics of online influence, how people earn it, and why companies urgently want to find it:

1. The availability of low-cost, high-speed Internet access and easy publishing tools such as Twitter, Facebook, and blogs has allowed anyone to create content, establish authority, and carve out a measure of influence on favorite subjects.

2. Not all influencers are created equal. Certain superconnectors ignite epidemics and are the epicenter of word-of-mouth influence. Combine them with these technological enablers, and a new era of powerful Citizen Influencers has begun.

3. Historical characteristics of influence such as authority, social proof, reciprocity, scarcity, consistency, and likability show up differently in the online world. The principles of social proof and reciprocity are particularly important in a digital environment where people may not be able to meet face-to-face and favors come with the ease of pushing a "like" button.

4. Humans crave authority. They want to know who they can turn to when decisions aren't clear. Plentiful badges of social

proof on the Internet such as the number of Twitter followers or Facebook friends can provide a shorthand indicator
of a person's status, especially when the amount of available information is overwhelming. The implication is that a
numerical marker of authority such as a Klout score can have
a legitimate impact on people's opinions about status and
influence even if the score doesn't necessarily reflect offline
reality or the system can be gamed.

5. Woven among and through traditional factors of influence is
   content. The ability to produce and/or aggregate compelling,
   meaningful, and entertaining content and move it virally
   through an engaged network is a means of establishing
   influence that is unique to the Internet. The talent to create
   and distribute content in its many forms can be a legitimate
   source of power apart from an individual's actual experience,
   ability, or personal accomplishments.

6. To the extent that we can measure the ability to create and
   move content, we can begin to quantify and measure one
   important aspect of online influence.

7. Identifying, nurturing, and activating these Citizen
   Influencers can provide incredibly powerful market insight
   to brands. Historically, finding these word-of-mouth leaders has been labor-intensive and expensive for marketers.
   Revolutionary new business models are emerging that allow
   companies to connect rapidly and inexpensively to topical
   niche influencers.

And that brings us, finally, to Klout and *your* number.

CHAPTER 7

Klout and the Evolution of Influence Marketing

JoeFernandez Joe Fernandez
Trying to get used to having my jaw wired totally shut. It's going to be a long couple months.
5 Dec 07

JoeFernandez Joe Fernandez
Trying to figure out the best way to measure a person's social influence on the web. Any ideas?
4 Mar 08

JoeFernandez Joe Fernandez
Planning world domination.
11 Mar 08

K lout is by far the market leader among more than a dozen companies that are attempting to quantify your level of online influence. According to public data and estimates, Klout receives more hits to its application programming interface (API) from third-party applications than all competitors combined.[1] With the bold tagline "the Standard for Influence," Klout hints at a day when the online and offline worlds will merge (more on that later).

---

1. An API is a set of programming instructions and standards for accessing web-based software. Companies release their APIs to the public so that other software developers can design products powered by their platform.

Klout compiles more than 100 different factors across dozens of social media platforms, pumps billions of pieces of data through its algorithms, and creates a personalized assessment of influence that ranges from 1 to 100. The world average is about 19. Someone with a score of 30 shows expertise, whereas a score of 50 or more means leadership and expert status.

And a perfect 100? That is reserved for one person alone: Justin Bieber. Many people think it's ludicrous that a teenage heartthrob could have more influence than Oprah or the president of the United States, but remember, this is a measure of *online* influence, and by all indications, when Justin tweets, his fans don't just listen, they act.

Klout scores are public, and everyone who participates on the social web has one whether he or she wants it or not. However, users must register on the Klout website and opt in to have any social media platform beyond Twitter included in their scores.

Klout doesn't measure all personal influence and never will. The company is, however, becoming increasingly adept at finding the people who are experts at creating, aggregating, and sharing content that moves online. And as we have seen by now, that's a legitimate marker for influence on the social web. People creating content is an action. Having a link clicked or a message retweeted is an effect. Klout, PeerIndex, and similar companies are attempting to quantify word-of-mouth influence on a *mass scale* by assessing and connecting millions of actions and effects every day. With teams of PhD-level scientists applying sociological, anthropological, and statistical rigor to its secret algorithms, Klout is trying to serve up marketing's Holy Grail: identification of the superconnectors, the Citizen Influencers, the epidemic igniters who can drive online buzz and make products move with a single blog post or video recommendation. These scientists are quantifying one sliver of online influence—and increasingly, with statistical predictability.

Although it's still in the silent movie stage of its technological development, the start-up company has already done a good enough job determining the consumer predilections of its millions of active users that major brands such as Disney, Chevrolet, Nike, and Revlon are integrating Klout's targeted marketing services with traditional advertising and marketing campaigns. In fact, Klout has generated so much interest in its influencer lists that it has been on a constant hiring binge to keep up with demand. Nearly 3,000 companies are using Klout's data in some form.

All this rapid success can be traced to a bored, frustrated young man sitting for hours on end playing on his computer and exploring social media sites because at that moment in his life, it was the only way he had to communicate with the outside world.

At age 17, Joe Fernandez, who was to become the founder of Klout, was suffering from intense head and stomach pains. He was diagnosed with a rare medical condition that could be resolved only by jaw surgery and literally wiring his mouth shut.

"I put the surgery off for years," Fernandez said. "I waited, hoping technology might get better and there would be like a lotion I could put on or something. But in 2007 the pain was getting worse, and I ended up having the surgery. I thought I could just power through it, but it was pretty hard. In fact, it was much harder than I ever imagined. My jaw was wired shut for two months, so to communicate, I either had to write stuff down or go on Twitter or Facebook because nobody could understand my mumbling.

"So I had this stir-crazy, drug-induced period of time in my 350-square-foot apartment in New York City. I was thinking about these social media tools I'm using to communicate, which at this point I am pretty much totally relying on for my life. And that intense experience really changed the way I thought about these tools. I began to notice that the people who trusted me the most would instantly follow what I was saying. I could tell them my opinion, and it would have some sort of impact on them.

"The other point that was interesting was that all this data was out there: The fact that Twitter and Facebook had an API and all of these other services had an API was pretty cool to me."

Locked up in his apartment for seemingly endless hours, Fernandez began to plot his ideas on an Excel spreadsheet: every social network he could find, every possible activity on those platforms that might signal influence. He saw patterns in the cells—connections—and the connections turned into equations.

An idea for a new company, a new way of marketing, was forming in his head, but the concept was really the culmination of a lifetime of entrepreneurial experimentation and failure.

The Young Entrepreneur

Fernandez grew up in a family that appreciated the value of taking a gamble. His grandfather was a hotel and casino magnate in Havana who moved his family to Las Vegas when the communist revolution shut down the gambling business in his country. Joe's father continued the family tradition, managing casino properties in Las Vegas, Lake Tahoe, and Atlantic City. Young Joe observed his father skillfully courting and befriending big spenders as a marketing manager for Caesars Palace, a lesson in networking that would be crucial to his development as an entrepreneur who had to call in a lot of favors to help his business survive.

As a teen, Fernandez envisioned a career in the casino business, but he also had an entrepreneurial bug from an early age. "Even in high school I had a lock on the used video game market," he said. "And in college I marketed music CDs through the players on the football team."

Fernandez attended the University of Miami (Florida) but couldn't settle on a career choice. "I changed my major like 20 times," he said. "I finished with an emphasis on economics, finance, and computer science, but I never actually graduated. You needed 126 credits, and I left with 140 in four years, but it was all over the place because I was always working on some side business and making pretty good money at it, too."

Fernandez had an opportunity to study English and political science at Oxford University for a year before landing his first job in 2000 with a technology consulting firm in Los Angeles. Little did he know that he was on the brink of a serious and extended personal collapse.

Within a few months of beginning his first real job, the white-hot Internet boom turned to bust and Fernandez was among the thousands of eager computer coders and tech consultants looking for work again. On the day of the World Trade Center nightmare, September 11, 2001, he learned that his younger brother—one of his best friends—had died unexpectedly in Iowa. With the nation's air system at a standstill, he jumped in his car and made the 1,800-mile drive from Los Angeles to Cedar Rapids, Iowa, alone and disconsolate.

After 10 months of unemployment, he could not find meaningful work and took a run at a childhood dream by using his meager savings to start a skateboard company, which failed in short order. His money was running out, he was on the verge of being evicted from his apartment, and his career prospects were bleak. To make ends meet, he took an entry-level technical support position. He hated the job, but his life was about to change for good.

Founding His First Company

In 2002, Fernandez met a retired psychologist who had an idea for streamlining the way public schools kept up with newly regulated reporting requirements for students. Fernandez, with the help of a few friends, started a company to build a computer program that would help school districts manage this paperwork-heavy process. As soon as the start-up had its product ready, it landed its first customer: the gigantic San Francisco Unified School District. With that bright start, they could not have foreseen that this would be their last customer.

"After that first sale, I really had visions of being a millionaire in a few months," he said. "But we could never sell another system. We couldn't figure out how to deal with the bureaucracy and politics of the school systems. We pushed and pushed for 18 months, bootstrapped it, and used every penny we had, but it became apparent that we weren't going anywhere with this idea."

In the end, the company salvaged its work by licensing the technology to other school system vendors that tracked lunch programs, special education efforts, and other student activities, a system that is still in place and generating revenue across 5,000 U.S. school districts.

Now 25, Fernandez was out of work once more, but he had several new weapons in his personal arsenal. He had learned what it was like to bootstrap a new business, lead a team of business partners, deal with the highs and lows of entrepreneurial life, and build a marketable product that was based on massive amounts of data. With the school project licensing deal, he finally had a little financial breathing room for his next venture.

With nothing left for him in California, Fernandez decided to follow a lifetime dream and move to New York City. He was soon using his natural networking skills to become part of the city's vibrant tech start-up scene.

"Pretty quickly after moving to New York I met three very smart guys who were starting a data company in the real estate space," he said. "Basically they were trying to aggregate all of the information around anything you would want to know if you were buying a house: the home sales in the neighborhood, the test scores for the school, the crime rate, whatever was useful in a real estate search. They would collect this information from any possible public source they could find, package it, and sell it to new real estate sites like Zillow, Trulia, and Coldwell Banker."

"The four of us were the executive officers of the company, and it was a really good experience," Fernandez said. "With the school database project, I had been the CEO but really had no clue about what I was doing. But with this venture, I was definitely riding the coattails of some really smart people and learning how to grow and run a business. In a year we grew to about 40 people doing $15 million in revenue, so this was becoming a substantial business entirely based on using other people's data. We were pulling free census information and county data, anything we could find. It was interesting to think about—building a profitable new business on free, publicly available data!

"My job at the time was to run product development, to think about what other types of relevant and useful data we could add to create new products. In 2006, social media platforms were starting to emerge, and it was natural for me to start examining how I might be able to bring all of these blogs and reviews into our system. I would play with any new tool I could find and think through the possibility of incorporating the data in a useful way that was applicable to real estate.

"This was when Web 2.0 and the social web were just taking off, and these innovations were so interesting, so exciting to me. I started to consider that maybe this is where I was meant to be. I enjoyed what I was doing, but I didn't have any real passion for real estate, so I started thinking about starting my own company.

"By late 2006, I had a couple of ideas. One would have been like a Foursquare/mobile kind of thing. I had another idea around restaurant reviews. I actually went to India, hired a team of developers, and tried building a few ideas on the side, but nothing really stuck. It appeared that I would be in real estate for the time being."

The Birth of Klout

"Then in 2007, I had the jaw surgery," Fernandez told me. "And my thinking about a new business model started to change a lot.

"I had so much time on my hands in my apartment, and as I experimented with these social media ideas, I started hacking something together that would be the first algorithm for influence. This idea for Klout just stuck with me. That was always the name: Klout. It was more about the idea of quantifying influence than the technology, and I couldn't shake it.

"When I got unwired, I quit the real estate company and did some consulting, but I was always working on this idea. I guess it became an obsession. I just couldn't stop thinking about the possibilities and realized that this was something I had to do. So in August 2008, I quit everything I was doing and went all-in on Klout."

Fernandez's first priority was to find a technical team to activate his idea, but he couldn't afford anybody in New York and couldn't persuade any of his friends to quit their jobs and bootstrap, so he turned to a group of developers in Singapore who had authored some of the software used by the real estate venture. "They had actually reported to me and I knew them really well, so I decided to hire those guys to help me with the first version of Klout," he said. "The time difference made it really hard to get anything done, so I went to Singapore for several months and crashed at the developer's house and worked in their office whenever I could to help build the first platform for Klout."

In less than six months, the software was ready to go, and the first version of Klout was launched on Christmas Eve 2008.

"It was pretty funny at the time," Fernandez said, "because if anyone registered, I had to manually calculate their score myself. So it was definitely a mess, but people were interested. The moment we launched, I tweeted my score. This caught the attention of some of my friends in New York, and it started to catch on among a small but rabid group of fans. To them, Klout was like ego crack.

"Just one week after I launched I was asked to present the idea at an important tech meet-up in New York City. I mean, it was kind of ridiculous to have this opportunity right out of the box. So January 4, 2009, I presented the idea publicly for the first time alongside CoTweet and StockTwits. I presented to about 500 or 600 people, and I was terrified. I really wasn't sure how to explain Klout. What was I going to say? That I had developed an algorithm that's going to decide how important everybody in the world is? How could I possibly say that? I've not achieved anything that would allow me to make a claim like that. There's nothing on my résumé that says I'm the one that should be allowed to make that decision. So here is what I told the crowd about market influence: 'Everybody who creates content has influence, and with Klout I want to understand who they influence and what they're influential about. It's not about the A list anymore. It's about *every person*.' And that resonated with the people in the audience. Klout was very crude back then—just one page, really—but I think they could see the vision that was behind it."

In early 2009, Fernandez returned to Singapore to supervise the next evolution of the product. Accompanying him was his friend

Binh Tran, a cofounder of the education software start-up, who quit his job to join the Klout venture full-time. Tran became the chief technical officer for Klout and continues to shepherd its development.

Klout on the Ropes

Between sleeping on the floor with his friends in Singapore and bootstrapping the new business from his tiny apartment, Fernandez was able to finance the first 18 months of the venture out of his own pocket. But investors would be necessary if Klout was going to avoid a death spiral. He needed to call on all his formidable networking skills to give the company a chance to survive from month to month.

"It was touch and go for a long time. I couldn't have made it through this period without a lot of help," he said. "The guys in Singapore and the company hosting us trusted me enough that they let us ride on our bills for a really long time. They would threaten to shut us off, and I would come up with $10,000 or $20,000 and we'd be cool again. If we would have had to pay them the full amount every month, well, it wouldn't have happened. I had to use all of the social and political capital I had, and I spent every penny of the money I had made from both of my previous companies, and still we were barely getting by. So I needed to meet people who could help. I decided that I needed to go to South by Southwest."

South by Southwest (SXSW), the annual tech event in Austin, Texas, is considered the World Series of start-ups. Tens of thousands of innovators and investors descend on the city each March, hoping to be the next big thing—or to discover it. During a stint in Singapore, Fernandez applied for a spot on one of the highly sought-after accelerator programs, in which a panel of judges helps find the coolest new start-up or web-based application. The Klout idea was accepted into the showcase. Fernandez was going to have his chance.

"This was a huge deal, an amazing opportunity. We needed this exposure because at that point we had just launched the company and literally had no money; I was begging and borrowing to keep Klout alive.

"I knew that once I got in front of that huge South by Southwest crowd with lots of investors and told them what we were doing, we would have funding the next day and everything would be perfect from there. So we show up, and we're given the 8 a.m. slot on the very last day. Not a popular time! The whole time I was there, all I did was stay in my hotel room to do coding and practice my two-minute presentation. That's all the time I had to save the company—two minutes! So I had all of this buildup, and when I arrived, there were four people in the audience. The microphone wasn't working. And the judges—Guy Kawasaki, Don Dodge, and Nova Spivack—are like, yeah, this is a dumb idea . . . NEXT. This was going to be our coming out party and . . . total crickets."

"We were out of money," Fernandez lamented. "This is early 2009, and the economy was terrifying. We built our platform initially on Twitter, and at that point people are still trying to decide if Twitter is a joke. I'm beginning to wonder, Can I really do this?

"As a last-ditch effort, I e-mailed the judges from the South by Southwest session to thank them for their time and their feedback and told them that I hoped we could talk some more sometime soon. Nova Spivack replied to me and said he thought our concept was interesting and offered to buy me coffee if I was ever in San Francisco. I replied back that I was going to be there the next week even though I had no specific plans to be there. We met, and I told him what I was thinking about Klout and what I was working on, and he thought it was really cool. He said he wanted to invest and wrote me a check that day. Our first angel investor! He also introduced me to an attorney to incorporate the company and also had me meet with a second investor. So we had our financing. We could keep going and slowly begin to grow.

"At that point, I didn't even own the Klout.com domain name. We were operating at Klout.net. So I was harassing the guy all the time who owned Klout.com, and he wanted $65,000 for the domain name and he told me to stop annoying him. So when I got that first check from Nova, I cashed it and I stalked the guy on Twitter and everywhere else I could find him. I saw from a tweet that he was at this restaurant, and I showed up with the cash and said, 'I'm the guy that's stalking you about this web address. I'm never going to leave you alone until I get it.' And I laid some cash on the table, and we did the domain transfer right there over lunch."

The Breakthrough

Money troubles continued to plague the young company despite the welcome infusion of cash. Ten months after the meeting with Spivack, Klout had no further interest from investors. "We were running on fumes the whole year," Fernandez said. "I pitched over 100 angel investors, and some would say, 'That's a dumb idea; Twitter's going to disappear.' Others would say, 'This is a good idea;

you should focus on the data side.' So I would revise my pitch for the next investor and focus on the data side, and then they would say, 'No, you should focus on the advertising piece,' so then my pitch would change for the next presentation. "

"I finally decided I needed to focus on my own vision for Klout," he said, "and I eventually attracted 37 angel investors, which is a lot—I don't know of any start-up that has that many. But we didn't attract any of the big names or these big shots that other tech companies have as investors. We sort of have this group of random, organic long-term investors, and over time we raised $1.5 million. That is what really got us going. We were able to hire a few people and move into an office in San Francisco."

The entrepreneur's networking instincts were keen even when it came to the location of the new company offices at 795 Folsom Street, the site of Twitter's headquarters.

"With our business model," he said, "it was important to be best friends with the Twitter guys." His theory was that by hanging out with executives at one of the hottest tech companies around, some of the magic could rub off. "I wanted to see who was visiting the Twitter office so I could pounce on them and meet them," said Fernandez. "And then I would invite them to swing by and visit us next door at Klout."

With an increasing number of fans in high places, the company easily raised another $1.5 million in May 2010 and seemed to be riding the wave of social media popularity.

"Social media and Twitter blew up, and the economy started to get better," Fernandez said. "Everyone, it seemed, began to realize that what we were doing might be important, and we started to get a lot of attention from the institutional VCs [venture capitalists]. In December 2010 we closed on $8.5 million from Kleiner Perkins. Basically, they are the Stanford or Harvard of venture capitalists. So to go from no interest in us at all to having the best VC in the world in less than a year was pretty exciting."

The Momentum for Social Scoring

The popularity of the social scoring system attracted attention from more than venture capitalists, however. Celebrities wanted in on the act as they vied for their own form of social proof and an elite status among the Twitterati.

"We get quite a few e-mails and calls from companies and celebrities trying to raise their score," Fernandez said. "We even got a call from the manager for Britney Spears. That was one of the first moments when it hit me as to where this might be going, the attention we were getting. I received an e-mail from her manager saying he was flying to San Francisco and wanted to meet me. It was a couple of people, him, a lawyer; they came by the office, we went out to lunch, and they really pressed me to know how to raise her Klout score: 'Why is Britney's Klout score lower than Lady Gaga's and Ashton Kutcher's?' This meeting just blew me away. Here was this worldwide celebrity who was aware of her Klout score and wanted to understand it and know how to change it."

"The timing is right for Klout," Fernandez claimed. "The importance of social networking broadly for individuals and companies has reached a tipping point, and we are in what I like to think of as an attention economy. With Facebook, people started using their real names, and as you start to use your own name online, your personal brand starts to matter. You can build your own influence like never before. All those things started happening around the same time Klout began its social credit score. It's been crazy for us because it is the right idea at the right time."

Although many people might get emotional about their Klout scores and the idea that they are being openly assessed, what those of us in the general public see on the Klout website is only the tip of the data iceberg. "The score is really just a small part of it," said Fernandez. "Below the surface we are analyzing data coming in from Twitter, Facebook, LinkedIn, and all of these other platforms, figuring out, is this about nutrition, or art, fashion, baseball?

"We're looking at all the content you create and analyzing what you're talking about. The algorithm will read your tweet or update and pick up mentions about music, baseball, fashion, or whatever your topic is. And then we'll look at 'When you talk about music, does your network respond?' If you talk about music or a concert and everybody goes crazy about what you say, that would be an indicator of influence, and that would show up in the Klout score. And as we process more and more of your content, it becomes more accurate over time.

"So we are defining what people are talking about, figuring out who responds to it, and how influential those people are. We're also looking at geography, like who in Philadelphia is the most influential about women's fashion or cooking."

"Another really powerful analysis we measure," he continued, "is the influence between every relationship. Like my mom is a good example. She's on Facebook, but the only reason she is there is to try to keep up with me and my sister. She's not trying to be influential, though she's really influential to us! So if she posts about where she's going on vacation, even though her Klout score is low, it's going to matter to us. So like in this example, we're trying to track who's influencing whom and on what topics.

"A practical example of what that could mean to advertisers would be, let's say there are three people who are influential to you and they are all talking about their vacations. So maybe in that context, it would be a good time to show you a JetBlue ad because there's a pretty good chance you might be starting to think about a vacation as well. In that way, we would be providing the ultimate in contextual advertising. Powerful to brands, helpful and timely to customers."

With this new opportunity to marry potential influencers to the products they loved, some of the world's most important brands took notice. In late 2010 the company piloted a program called Perks, which allowed client companies to offer free gifts, discounts, upgrades, and other benefits to influencers by topic. The initiative was incredibly successful, straining the start-up's resources. Klout quadrupled its workforce in 12 months to keep up with demand. A notable hire in 2011 was the company's first chief revenue officer, Yahoo! veteran Tim Mahlman. Klout is one of the few social media start-ups to monetize its offering so quickly.

As important as these campaigns have been to the company's cash flow, additional revenue is coming in from the nearly 3,000 API partners, including the *Huffington Post*, Seesmic, and HootSuite. Software programs using the Klout scores as part of their own product offerings make tens of billions of "calls" to the Klout API every month, 500 times more than its nearest competitor.

Another strategic focus for the company has been adding platforms such as Facebook, YouTube, blogs, and LinkedIn to its traditional Twitter database, allowing the company to reach more social media users, collect more data, and provide a richer influencer profile. How many social media platforms will be added in the future? "As many as possible. All of them," said Fernandez. The idea from the original spreadsheet is still alive.

With the company's meteoric growth have come inevitable questions about leadership and the future. "Even when we had just five people in the company, I was really questioning if I was the right person to keep leading," Fernandez offered. "We even discussed it at the board level. But I've learned not to worry so much about experience that I don't have because we are creating something brand new. Nobody has been here before, and no one is as capable as I am with what we're inventing. I'm pretty comfortable with where we are. I am sometimes stumbling through as a CEO, but there's no reason to hide that. It's challenging in a very good way.

"Although we've grown a lot, the vision really hasn't changed. One of the first VCs I pitched—and one of the first to turn us down—re-sent me the e-mail with the original description of what we were going to do. You could cut and paste it into what I say today and it's the same. It's pretty crazy to go from this one idea that was just the right idea at the right time."

It looked like Klout was finally on its way. Companies were clamoring to use its rating systems. Money was starting to flow in the right direction. Fernandez was assembling a world-class team of experts to take his company to the next level. Although it was not quite yet "the Standard for Influence," Klout certainly seemed to be dominating its niche.

There was only one problem: What do you do when many of the same powerful influencers that the company is trying to identify and nurture despise you?

CHAPTER 8

Controversy and Turmoil

ALL_CAPS David Hicks
Klout is the drunk dad of social media: you hate him but still
seek his approval.
6 Jun

While Klout rocketed ahead on an upward trajectory,
its reputation was starting to take a hit from many
irate social media users who loathed the idea of being
publicly rated and compared.

Quirks in the company's early programming awarded astronom-
ical influence scores to fake "bot" Twitter accounts, created wild
weekly swings in influence scores, and assigned silly and irrelevant
influence topics to people. Popular bloggers railed at the real and
perceived invasion of privacy and complained that the company was
using information gleaned from millions of public accounts—without an option to opt out or manage privacy settings—for economic
gain. Fernandez and his company took a beating from many of the
same Citizen Influencers they were trying to recognize and celebrate.

Perhaps the apex of the anti-Klout frenzy occurred in late 2011
when the company reset its algorithm in an effort to improve its
accuracy, resulting in many precipitous declines in scores and an
outcry from even Klout loyalists. A typical response among the
1,500 comments on the Klout blog: "22-point drop. My immediate
reaction? Unlinked all services, revoked access from Twitter, and
sent them an e-mail asking them to permanently delete my account.
I've had it. Klout is dead to me. I'll be waiting for a new service to
come along that actually respects its users."

"Some people have reacted pretty negatively to the idea of being
rated around influence," Fernandez admitted. "I would say even
violently so."

111

Although algorithmic rating systems for websites and blogs are commonly accepted flaws and all, people have reacted quite differently when they are applied to *personal* scores.

Take this reaction from Kimmo Linkama, a marketing and creative consultant in Baltic Europe:

> *Pardon my French, but I'm really pissed off. As if your worth to humankind is suddenly being determined by some geeks inventing clever algorithms. And* perks? *For heaven's sake, they could as well give perks to people who have red hair, wear glasses, or like prawns. Social media presence is becoming seriously—and dangerously—overrated.*

Or this one from Shelby Stanley, who commented on my blog:

> *This takes superficiality to the max! I can't stand that we've become such narcissistic digital fiends. I can understand active participation within the social networking world as a way to connect and contact, however, implementing a system like this that celebrates one's digital influence over something as solid as human connection makes me feel uneasy about the future and our ability to generate healthy, social relationships. I like to think I'm a people person, but am I less of one if I don't measure up in Facebook friends? Oh dear. Oh dear oh dear oh dear.*

To many, this whole trend is starting to feel a lot like high school. The people with high Klout scores are the cool kids, and the reaction is that either we want to be with the cool kids too or we resent the whole idea.

But in addition to the very emotional and visceral reactions of being rated in a public way, there are many legitimate concerns about the social scoring trend, privacy, the underlying methodology, and its implications.

Spammers, Hackers, and Bots (Oh My!)

I dread the day that the masses learn to control their influence scores.
—**PAM MOORE**, CEO, FruitZoom, Inc.

A challenge for any Internet start-up is fending off the inevitable attacks from those who want to game the system. In 2009 Twitter was almost brought to its knees by the onslaught of fake accounts cluttering the system and annoying its customers. Facebook, the largest and most important social network, is a natural target for hackers seeking to exploit holes in the system. Quora skyrocketed to popularity in 2010 when it was Scobleized, only to find itself deluged by self-serving posts from people trying to earn credit in the never-ending battle to optimize search engine standings.

Unfortunately, where corruption can occur, corruption will occur, and any new company had better be prepared to scale to meet the onslaught. This issue has proved to be a challenge for Klout, resulting in some public embarrassments. One of the difficulties the company has faced involves culling fake accounts that can show up as social media Klout superstars.

Matt Ridings, the founder of MSR Consulting, notes that he has a slightly lower Klout score than the mayor of his hometown of St. Louis. Both of them rank lower on Klout than @common_squirrel, a Twitter account whose content consists solely of posts such as "acorn" and "jump jump jump jump."

Matt Owen, a social media manager at Econsultancy, put Klout to the test. Could a fake account really have influence? Matt set up an automated Justin Bieber news stream as an experiment. The Twitter account, unassociated with any real person or human activity, simply amalgamated RSS feeds from various celebrity news sites and pumped them out at the rate of one every two minutes. He could then test the performance of a fake account loosely associated with a celebrity with his personal Klout score, which was derived from a legitimate and consistent stream of news and engagement.

"Given the vast difference in these two accounts, it stands to reason that the 'real' one should be far more influential than the fake one," he said. "On my account I reply, retweet, link out to relevant content. In short, I engage on a one-to-one basis and try to be a half-decent digital citizen, while my bot account does none of these. You can shout at it to quit spamming you all you like—it doesn't care."

After a few weeks, the results were in.

Both accounts had accrued a similar number of followers (there are obviously a lot of Justin Bieber fans out there), and the Klout scores for the real person and the bot were about the same. Further, Klout described the bot's influence level this way:

You actively engage in the social web, constantly trying out new ways to interact and network. You're exploring the eco-system and making it work for you. Your level of activity and engagement shows that you "get it" and we predict you'll be moving up.

This conclusion is impossible, of course: The bot doesn't engage with anyone, it doesn't network, it doesn't "get" anything.

"On the surface, this was a bit of fun," Owen said. "It lets you know if you're doing things right or not and drops hints to help you improve. If you are using these figures for business, though, it soon becomes apparent that the metrics being used are woefully inadequate and possibly detrimental."

"Tools and apps simply cannot compare with human input," he said. "When finding influencers you want to engage, by all means look at the big numbers, but only as an initial benchmarking technique. Once you've found some likely candidates, you can spend time examining profiles manually.

"To put this in context, ask yourself, Would you hire a new head of marketing based purely on the amount of recommendations they received on LinkedIn? Of course not; you'd interview them, and if you want to succeed at social [media], you'll need to be prepared for a lengthy vetting process."

Over time, Klout and other start-up companies measuring influence will undoubtedly improve their processes and attempt to correct obvious tactics that are used to embarrass the system. But there is a darker, more elusive threat to any formula-based online business: armies of people willing to help you cheat the system for a few bucks.

The Economics of Cheating

The Internet's underground economy of cheating has become big business. As both the financial and psychological benefits of having a high Klout score rise, so will the stakes as people create business models specifically designed to cheat. In fact, it's already happening. There are cells of people across the world dedicated to beating the system, whatever that system might be.

James D (he wanted to withhold his last name) has had a hard time making ends meet holding down just his day job but has found a profitable new business in creating false Twitter accounts pre-loaded with thousands of followers to sell on eBay. By using lists of accounts known to automatically "follow back," James can semiautomate the process so that he makes money even when he is away from the computer. "I chose to enter this business because I have learned how to make these accounts efficiently and I needed to make some extra cash," he said.

He has found many people willing to fork over money just to have the social proof of a large Twitter following even though the customers don't know a single person on the list. "Anyone trying to get exposure for their product or business and even people who just want to get a large amount of followers to become more popular on Twitter buy followers from me. I can get between seven and eight dollars for every thousand followers." The lists are easily available on eBay. Of course, many of the followers on the accounts are not even real people, but that doesn't seem to be a significant factor if the goal is social proof.

Just about any online rating system can be gamed. One scam plaguing the hospitality industry is fake hotel reviews. The fake reviews undermine the credibility of nearly every travel-related website these days. Buyers can simply find individuals on Craigslist and other sources to populate the web with positive reviews. The problem is so widespread that it became the focus of a Cornell University research study.

Students and faculty developed software capable of recognizing patterns in reviews that were known fakes. The software compared 320 gushy hotel write-ups produced by fake accounts with 320 authentic reviews that appeared on TripAdvisor, where writers are required to have booked their trips through the site. It turns out that fake reviewers tend to use more verbs and less punctuation and focus more on family activities than on the actual hotels. Once the software was trained, researchers tested it on the reviews in their database, and the software could guess correctly 90 percent of the time. Humans can manage this feat about half the time.

Can you game your appearance of influence the same way? Yes, it can be done, and it is done on a regular basis. Autoposting, tweet blitzes, buying followers, trading votes, inviting spam bot interaction, and fake Foursquare mayorships can all help pump up a fictitious Klout score. For many people, the web isn't the real world, so what's wrong if you cheat a little? And when there are jobs, trips, merchandise, and other perks on the line, people are willing to do just about anything to gain favor in the system.

Black Market Influence

An example of how these systems can be gamed is offered by my friend Tom (not his real name), who went down a dark path to try to win a new iPad through a B2B company's Facebook contest. Most Facebook contests are relatively simple and are designed to attract new fans and followers to a company page. In this contest, Tom simply had to post a photograph on a company Facebook page and get the most friends to like it to win the coveted prize of the newly released Apple tablet computer.

Tom worked his network diligently as he asked friends and family members to like his photograph. In no time, he was comfortably in the lead. Then, with just a few days before the end of the contest, another participant, Karen, came from far behind to take the lead with a few hours to go.

"It didn't make sense," Tom said, "so I dug into it a little closer. When I looked at the people who had liked her image, I found something interesting. Not only were most of the people from all over the world, they were not actually connected to her through Facebook! I couldn't figure it out. How did she manage to extend her network, and her influence on these people, so far and so quickly? There was something wrong."

Tom probed further. Google searches produced links to Facebook fan pages devoted to vote trading. Vote trading pages are based on the idea that a person will vote for or like your item if you will like theirs. "On that one-to-one level, it's essentially fine," Tom said. "The problem comes when you start seeing people trading 10, 100, or even 300 votes." He found that this trading was all accomplished through an underground economy driven by fake Facebook accounts.

"There are groups of people, mainly in Third World countries, who do nothing but help people cheat at contests, and they do it as a way of earning a meager living," Tom said. "There are essentially two workflows in these so-called companies. The first group creates and fleshes out bogus profiles. Many times the list of visible friends is just their dummy account. Most of the time the fake accounts portray themselves as female, with limited information in the profile. People are more likely to trust and interact with a female account, it seems.

"The second group turns and burns. They take the bogus accounts and put them into action in two different uses. One account will be the 'front' account—the 'living account.' This is the one that contacts real users and interacts with them to negotiate how many votes will be traded at once. Many of these accounts might eventually get flagged by Facebook and suspended for suspicious activity. In that event, a new account is then simply brought to the front to be used in its place. The supply is endless, of course. Many times it will even appear to be the exact same account but with a different e-mail attached to it. The remaining accounts will be used to place votes or likes.

"So my initial thought was, I can beat this lady at her own game. I was upset that I had worked so hard only to see somebody buy their way into the lead. And that's how I started down the path of gaming the contest. I'm not proud of it, but it happened."

The race was on, and his competitive juices were flowing. Tom even created dummy accounts of his own so that he could offer more to trade with the vote sellers. The contest spiraled into a virtual slugfest. Tom would gain 500 or more votes, and Karen would come back with 600 votes. Tom would keep using his fake accounts to help him until they got flagged and suspended by Facebook. He quickly created more and more replacement accounts; surely his rival was doing the same?

"It got crazy," he said. "It was ridiculous. I couldn't believe what I was doing. I was trashing this honest company's pages with hundreds of spammy likes from people who didn't even exist. The moral issues were weighing on me. What kind of an example was I setting? I was participating in a fraudulent activity to win a chunk of metal. So I gave up. I let her win."

All the tactics mentioned in these examples—buying a Twitter following, automating and publishing content that you've never seen, and using fraudulent practices to get more Facebook likes—can also directly or indirectly contribute to a higher Klout score.

Gaming for Klout

Glen Gilmore, a New Jersey–based attorney and marketing strategist, sees gaming tactics in his daily engagements. "The problem with Klout? Like most things in social media, it can be gamed. How? Notice some folks on Twitter suddenly getting terribly chatty with other users with mass followings? Prolonged conversations that should be taken to a private setting? Gaming under way! Spend some extra time on your follow/following ratio and you'll get to boost your Klout score as well. When a service that can be gamed becomes the gold standard, real clout loses to gamed Klout."

Keeping the metric's algorithm cloaked in mystery is unavoidable if Klout and other companies are to guard their investments against abuse. Just as national treasuries use special papers, holograms, and watermarks to protect against the counterfeiting of money, influence systems must do their best to disguise their algorithms to prevent counterfeiting of that valuable online currency, social proof. At the same time, this mystification impedes clear assessments of the scoring system's validity by companies that authentically want to understand the process, and impedes the efforts of honest users who sincerely want to understand the effectiveness of their online presence. As a compromise, some social scoring services are providing timelines that users can use to track their social media activity against scores, but there is probably no long-term way to assure both transparency of information and integrity of the algorithms.

"Gaming the system is a legitimate concern," said Shripal Shah, who has had extensive experience managing Klout-based marketing programs for major consumer brands. "In traditional marketing, if a brand is going after a spokesperson, you may look at an established metric like an E score or a Q score. Klout seems to be the metric right now for the everyday person. I don't think there's truly another more valid social metric, but gaming the number is a problem. It's something you have to live with on the Internet to some degree or another.

"A lot of brands are spending money trying to get 1 million Facebook fans," he said. "Are they not spending money just to get a number? Isn't that kind of the same thing? You have to look at context—is the Klout number any worse than what's already out there? Some of the criticism of Klout scores may be valid, but I trust they are going to be constantly improving and minimizing the issue. If it comes to the point where the gaming is overtaking the legitimacy, you've got to find a new metric."

Social Media May Be an Ineffective Place to Exert Influence

Sadly, it seems that Klout is becoming a people scoring tool that isn't based in reality. Seriously, is it possible to tweet, Facebook, LinkedIn, blog, and check in one's way to the C-suite? Of course not.
                          —**BETH HARTE**, marketing professional and university educator

I have a fairly well-established social media presence. Klout would consider me an influencer in this field, and my blog *{grow}* is among the most-read marketing sites in the world. I am creating valuable content that moves virally through the Internet every day. So, the social proof associated with my success attracts some attention, and I get requests from folks asking for Twitter help every day, usually to retweet a notable blog post or perhaps in support of their charities. I'm glad to help when I can, but I'll let you in on a little secret: When you ask online friends to take an action beyond the easy task of hitting a computer keyboard button, when they really need to get their skin in the game and *do* something, it usually doesn't work.

Some people look at my social proof badges and imagine that I can be their gateway to fame and influence. I've been around long enough to know that these factors do not necessarily translate into offline success. Even when I ask people to take action on something I really believe in, typically little action occurs. This is not a matter of being humble or gracious. It is simply the truth. When I tweet something, it rarely results in tangible action.

This phenomenon was also noted in Tom Webster's fine *Brand Savant* blog. In an extraordinary measure, he personally contacted every Klout-infested A-list blogger he could think of to help him with a New Zealand earthquake charity appeal.

Tom calculated that the "reach" of his message easily exceeded 600,000. Out of that number, his appeal received 389 clicks and 10 submissions to his cause. Tom admits there were some complications that could have depressed the number, but he pithily states that this conversion rate, compliments of some of the world's greatest Twitter influencers, was significantly lower than what would be expected from a random pop-up ad.

Perhaps the most extreme example of this lack of tangible response was the case of the missing book sales.

Megan Garber of the Nieman Journalism Lab reported that Alyssa Milano—known for being on the *Who's the Boss* television series and more recently for being a celebrity presence on Twitter—sent out a somewhat unusual tweet to her nearly 1.2 million followers: a link to the Amazon page of a book called *Connected: The Surprising Power of Our Social Networks and How They Shape Our Lives* by Nicholas Christakis and James H. Fowler.

For a book like *Connected*, written by social scientists and built on some heady academic research, you'd think that a message broadcast from a heavily followed Twitter account would lead to a huge spike in sales. Amplification, after all, comes from size: The more followers a person has, the more people will see a message and potentially retweet it and thus the more people will potentially act on it. This setup had all the makings of a viral success story.

How many extra books were sold in the wake of that million-follower tweet?

None. Literally not one. In fact, in the days and weeks after Milano's tweet, the book's sales actually declined. The actress's follower numbers in this case hadn't been a force for much of anything. "At least with respect to the influence of behavior," Christakis noted, "these Twitter links are weak."

But maybe it was just a Hollywood thing. Although Alyssa is a social media celebrity as well as the television variety, it's fair to assume that the overlap between Milano followers and the universe of people who might buy an academic book by two professors would be low. Christakis and Fowler next asked Tim O'Reilly, a respected new media publisher with nearly 1.5 million followers, to send the *Connected* link out to his feed.

The result? One book sale.

I've also had my blog posts tweeted by Alyssa Milano and other Twitterati, and although it definitely leads to a short-term spike in pageviews, it has never resulted in any measurable difference in new blog subscribers. In fact, after Guy Kawasaki (Klout score 85, Twitter followers 375,000) tweeted my post five times in 24 hours, my blog reader subscriptions went down.

On Twitter, no one can hear you scream.

Social Media Links Are Weak Links

Although there has been little serious research so far on these social media connections and offline influence, these examples are illustrations of what many consider the weak links of social media connections. Social networks are effective at increasing participation by lessening the level of motivation that participation requires. It takes no effort to click a "like" button, for example. But it takes more investment to act on a person's influence and buy a book, show up at a rally, or contribute to a charity.

Shelly Kramer is one of the most popular business personalities on the social web and is regularly featured on lists of the most powerful women in the new media. However, she's skeptical about what it really means.

"Being regarded as powerful on the Internet doesn't really mean all that much most of the time," she said. "Have you ever tried to get somebody on the Internet to actually do something? People will share your content all day long, but try to get somebody to give to a charity, hire somebody because they do good work, make a video, or take an action that requires them to get up out of their chairs—that's elusive.

"I read an article about how to be more effective on Facebook. The author's advice was to avoid asking people to do anything. Well, as marketers, our job is to *get* people to do something! So it's a weird business. Sure, maybe it's easy to get somebody to like a Facebook page, but even getting them to leave a blog comment is hard work."

In his much-debated *New Yorker* article "Small Change," Malcom Gladwell noted that the Facebook page of the Save Darfur Coalition has 1,282,339 members who have donated an average of 9 cents apiece. The next biggest Darfur charity on Facebook has 22,073 members who have donated an average of 35 cents. Help Save Darfur has 2,797 members who have given on average 15 cents. A spokesperson for the Save Darfur Coalition told *Newsweek,* "We wouldn't necessarily gauge someone's value to the advocacy movement based on what they've given. This is a powerful mechanism to engage this critical population. They inform their community, attend events, volunteer. It's not something you can measure by looking at a ledger."

In other words, Facebook activism succeeds not by motivating people to make a real sacrifice but by motivating them to do the things that people do when they are not motivated enough to make a real sacrifice, such as click a mouse on a like button.

This issue is a complicated one that may vary by personality, industry, and subject matter. Paradoxically, there is no question that the weak ties connecting people on Twitter and Facebook coalesced into a cataclysmic force for change in Egypt and much of the Middle East during the Arab Spring of 2011. These disparate social media whispers grew into a uniting force that inspired people to risk their lives in a remarkable two-year social media collaboration that began with bloggers calling for labor strikes and resulted in an energetic youth movement that toppled dictators.

Not only did social media enable Citizen Influencers to ignite an epidemic, it united an entire region of the world, shared best practices between protest groups, and kept the revolutionaries one step ahead of government countermeasures. When protesters in Cairo's Tahrir Square faced off against government forces, they were prepared with this Facebook lesson from supporters in Tunisia: "Advice to the youth of Egypt: Put vinegar or onion under your scarf for tear gas."

Thus, even if we accept that weak social media connections such as Facebook friends and Twitter followers could possibly drive dramatic real-life behavior such as registrations, attendance, sales, and even a revolution, how would we know for sure? With the certainty of statistically valid measurement, how do we know that something said online is going to result in an offline behavior? That connection is elusive, at least for now, and that leads to the next challenge.

Can Online Measurements Be a True Indication of Offline Influence?

Algorithms can probably measure "influence" as well as they can measure the truth.

—**JACOB VARGHESE**, president, Brandbite Media

This line of questioning is also known as the Oprah effect.

Tom Webster, a world-class questioner and VP of Edison Research, illustrates this concern when he asks, "Is it even possible to measure online influence, divorced from offline influence?"

"If a Klout score is truly focused solely upon online behavior," he goes on to say, "then Oprah's Klout score should be far less than 65, since she has only 134 Tweets and follows just 19 people. Clearly her *offline* influence, not her online behavior, is solely responsible for her higher Klout score. Yes, she has well over 4 million followers, but certainly not by dint of her Twitter ability!

"If offline influence is the goal here, then surely someone so influential as Malcolm Gladwell should pull better than a Klout score of 25. While Gladwell does not participate in Twitter, he is certainly discussed. When his *New Yorker* article 'The Revolution Will Not Be Tweeted' was published, it dominated online discussions for weeks. Shouldn't that create a high influence score?"

"If Klout is working toward capturing that kind of influence," Webster said, "including citations, searches, and trackbacks, then they are building something very impressive indeed.

"They may very well be the closest to cracking that nut, but there are a lot of offline confounding variables. The social media universe is just too small to serve as the basis for those conclusions, and the whole process strikes me as inductive (rather than deductive) reasoning. After all, if [business author] Seth Godin and Malcolm Gladwell have chosen not to interact on Twitter, then perhaps it is Twitter, and not those gentlemen, that is unimportant.

"One of my favorite definitions of science is this: If you can formulate a hypothesis and then test it, it is science. If you cannot test it, it is *faith*. How does one test an influence score? How do you know, in other words, if you got it right?"

"Assigning validation to Klout alone is dangerous," said Robert Scoble. "The system is biased in favor of people who put a lot of content into the system and who are able to get a lot of people to retweet and follow. Maybe that's a good attribute in somebody you're going to hire, but not always, and we've seen that kind of thing reflected in society. Is Rebecca Black really a better singer than Adele? That's debatable, but she can certainly move content. Her videos are everywhere! That might make her Klout score higher as a reflection of short-term popularity, but it's not necessarily a reflection of ability."

Another aspect of social scoring systems that has raised both suspicion and ire is the silliness that sometimes results from the blips and bleeps in the Klout algorithms. Most people have seen charts showing that they are being influenced by people they have never heard of. One of the most mysterious puzzlements is when Klout determines that you are an influencer on seemingly random topics.

"For about eight or nine weeks I was listed as being influential about lamps," said Sam Fiorella of Toronto's Sensei Marketing. "Lamps? I know nothing about lamps and could not even remember mentioning lamps in a tweet. So I literally went back through thousands of tweets and did not find the word *lamp*. I copied the tweets and put them through a word search. No lamps. Not once. What does that mean? How could I possibly be influential about lamps?"

Sam admits that Klout appears to have fixed many of these early problems, but for many people, silly mistakes like that made the company a lightning rod for criticism.

"A bunch of my online friends and connections thought it'd be fun to say I'm influential about sheep," wrote blogger Danny Brown, "since I wrote a blog post about sheep telling the shepherd to flock off (correlating to loyal readers questioning the quality of A-list blogs). Klout now lists me as being superinfluential about sheep, but I'm pretty sure if I tried talking to farmers about wool and shearing, I'd put them out of business quicker than you can say baaaaa!"

Despite the obvious disconnect from many true indicators of offline influence, the Klout score can still be a useful indicator, according to many business professionals, including the technologist Neelu Modali of SoMeGo, who is studying adaptations of Klout scores for potential applications to governmental processes.

"Klout doesn't necessarily measure a direct action on a given day," Modali said. "It doesn't measure the influence you have on your daughter, for example. But in some cases it can be applicable in the context of how business and trade are *probably* going to be conducted. The whole philosophy is that your online reputation, or your *capacity* to influence, your probability to influence, is going to be increasingly defined by metrics. There's no doubt about that trend.

"A good correlation might be like when the credit score formula was first devised. A person might complain about this score: 'Hey, this number doesn't represent my honor as a person or my capacity to repay a debt! How can this number accurately predict my intention or ability to pay this back when we've not had this long-term relationship?' But a credit score is an indicator of probable behaviors, isn't it? Klout is just an example of this same principle applied to business and trade on this new social web."

"The difference between online and offline influence is definitely a challenge," said Klout's Joe Fernandez. "We get a lot of flak for giving Justin Bieber a higher Klout score than Barack Obama. But if you look at the rate of engagement that Bieber drives, the data is pretty clear. Sure, most of the people who interact with him are 14-year-old girls, but the order of magnitude more engagement he drives is staggering. That doesn't mean he has the power to invade foreign nations or fix health care, but *in his category*, there is no question that Justin Bieber makes things happen. If he posts a tweet asking people to fill a theater, it gets filled. If he encourages people to visit a website, they do. He has a very loyal, responsive group of followers."

Is Social Scoring Driving Corrupt Behaviors?

Although Klout sounds like a good idea on the surface, some of the implications I've seen in the real world haven't been so pretty. For example, at the last agency I was at there was no good way to judge if Twitter was being used effectively for clients. Along comes Klout, and managers began to say, "Why is the Klout score down?" "Get our Klout score up!" with no real business case or objectives to go along with it.

—**BRANDON CROKE**, marketing manager, Inigral

Zach Bussey, a 25-year-old consultant cited in a *Wall Street Journal* article, started taking a proactive approach to managing his score. "It is an ego thing," he was quoted as saying.

One of the services he turned to was TweetLevel, created by the public relations firm Edelman. Similar to Klout, it grades users' influence, popularity, trust, and engagement on a scale of 1 to 100. He decided to try to improve his score by boosting the ratio of people who follow him to the number he follows, and so he halved the number of people he was following to 4,000. His TweetLevel score rose about 5 points, and his Klout score jumped from 51 to 60. "The change gave me more legitimacy," he said. But, he warns, you can't get lazy: "If you go on vacation for a week and can't tweet every hour of the day, you better be prepared to see your scores drop."

Although it may seem incredible that people would think about missing out on a vacation to keep a Klout score up, that was exactly the sentiment expressed by some of my blog readers when I wrote a tongue-in-cheek article about how my Klout score dropped when I went on a two-week vacation. The conclusion, I said (sarcastically), is that we need to stay put.

To my amazement, people took that advice seriously. Some readers started questioning the wisdom of going on vacations after working so hard to build their social media presence.

"This is what I was worried about," one reader wrote me. "I have to go out of the country on a long business trip. What's going to happen to my Klout score?"

The web is filled with stories about all-night Twitter blitzes, internal company competitions, and blog posts dedicated to teaching people how to beat the system. Modern snake oil salespersons are already setting up shop as Klout coaches.

There are even elitists willing to bestow their high Kloutness on you and your customers. "There's an interesting sort of ecosystem developing with some people who get their Klout scores in the 70s," said Naveen Krishnamurthy, president/CEO of RIVA Solutions, Inc. "People are putting themselves up for hire based on their Klout score. They are basically putting it out there saying, 'Engage with us and we can help play your audience.' It's even showing up in our recruiting process. There's been this mentality of 'my Klout score is above 70, so there's this price tag for me to be associated with you because I can make a lot of noise and get you a lot of followers.'

"For some people, it has taken two years to build that intrinsic value as part of their personal brand, and now they want to be paid for it. They're also telling me that if I hire them, they won't do anything or put themselves in the social media stream for my company in a way that would hamper their ability to keep their score up."

"I know someone who was part of the Virgin Airlines Klout schwag, and Klout could set her on fire and she wouldn't say a negative word about them," said Shelly Kramer. "She wants *more* opportunities and wouldn't damage her social cred for the world. I think this is part of the danger of this scoring business. There will always be people who are willing to sell their souls for a few shillings. Me, I'm going to say what I want, when I want, where I want, and Klout score be damned."

"Social media is meant to be a place where transparency and authenticity reign supreme," added Judi Samuels, a Toronto-based marketing and communications professional. "As soon as you start grading/scoring people, you take away the desire to be authentic and impose the desire to compete. If you are only jostling for a higher score, are you being real?"

Dr. Jon Buscall is one of Scandinavia's leading marketing consultants and teachers and sees a threat of Klout becoming a system that helps undermine individuality: "A favorite author, Jean Baudrillard, envisioned a society driven by the processes of late capitalism where we are locked in to a network of communications where we have problems positioning 'the self.' To my mind, this is Klout: an algorithm that sweeps us up even if we try and resist, reducing us to an easily digestible figure of apparent worth. We can't position ourselves and are positioned by the 'late-capitalist network of communication.'

"From a business point of view Klout could potentially (will?) shape business decisions and to my mind echoes what Baudrillard talks about in terms of the crisis of the self: My personal recommendation becomes nothing compared to the recommendation of the system (i.e., Klout)."

Social Scoring Is Creating a New Caste System

Should [social scoring] come to pass, I will be obliged to oppose it by any means necessary. What you describe here is nothing less than an attempt to define and control the separation between the haves and the have-nots in a way that is fundamentally anti-American. The only thing that stops me from taking this seriously is that I trust my fellow citizens to oppose something like this as vehemently as I do.

—**ERIC HARE**, marketing consultant

There is nothing that presses people's hot buttons more than an appearance of preferential treatment, and that is exactly what social scoring systems are meant to accomplish—reward the elite, or at least the perceived elite. And that makes people angry.

Many global societies value—at least in theory—the idea that we are all created equal. We should all be able to be seated at a nice restaurant, buy tickets to a popular concert, or win a contest. But in the world of social scoring and Klout Perks, this economy is turned upside down. Today a digital grading system based on tweets, followers, and status updates can be your path to popularity, career advancement, opportunity, and financial reward.

Some social media platforms will even allow you to filter your followers and their content by the highest Klout scores. This portends the possibility of creating an "engagement ceiling" that keeps newcomers with low scores out of the picture.

Although the Klout algorithm is a tightly kept secret, founder Joe Fernandez has stated on several occasions that engaging with people with higher scores will have a tendency to raise your score. If this is taken to an extreme, nobody will want to engage with newbies. In fact, nobody will even see the newbies if they are filtered out. Not only would this emerging caste system reward only those perceived as powerful, it would shut down the young, the newcomers, the uninitiated, and those with something better to do than spend their day on Twitter and Facebook.

This mistreatment might extend into the offline world as well. Companies already are making outsized efforts at servicing cranky Twitter complainers, popular bloggers, and prolific reviewers. But what's coming is a bigger picture of an individual's media footprint—servicing customers on the basis of influence—and customer service organizations are already adjusting to handle the situation delicately.

Salesforce.com, a leading CRM services provider, is now including Klout scores in its software to help companies parse through the high volume of social media traffic to determine who should get priority responses. The software allows companies to set conditions for incoming social media traffic and apply automated responses like coupons or special offers based on social scores.

The Privacy Firestorm

Klout is like a vampire showing itself in the sunlight.
—**MARTIJN LINSSEN**, founder of We Wire People

The basic economic model for most social media platforms is to collect as much personal information about people as possible and leverage that database to sell targeted advertising. One common characterization of this strategy is that "if the product is free, *you* become the product."

Google+ was created and launched in 2011 largely because Google was losing market share of personal information to Facebook. According to a Citi Investment Research & Analysis report, the amount of time Americans spent with Facebook as a percentage of their total online experience rose from about 5 percent at the end of 2009 to about 15 percent by mid-2011. Google's share was approximately 10 percent throughout that period.

This is a high-stakes game. In every moment of this attention economy, personal information is being shared that will eventually turn into advertising dollars. More data equals better targeting, which results in higher revenue.

These new media giants are recording, dissecting, and distributing a running log of our lives. In countries such as the United States, Facebook is even able to track the activities of nonmembers who view their pages for any reason through cookies that track online behavior. This practice has generated a backlash of privacy sentiment that culminated in a congressional investigation in the United States and regulation in some countries.

The use of this personal information extends beyond advertising. Insurance companies are monitoring Twitter and Facebook to find reasons to raise premiums. One executive recruiter told me that a person's "social graph" may be more important in the vetting process than a résumé. Nonprofit organizations are balancing privacy concerns against this unprecedented access to personal data to create "rich lists" of potential donors.

Of course Klout is using this data to create complex personal profiles, too. The only difference is that instead of doing it secretly, they are openly telling the world what they are doing and why.

This unusual visibility of the inner workings of the attention economy makes the company a lightning rod for vocal privacy advocates. As Klout's business profile grew and commercial success began to draw attention to the company, the accuracy and usefulness of its rating system, the inability to opt out of the program easily, and the mistakes it made as it iterated in a very public manner generated a firestorm of criticism.

In late 2011 the outrage from critics reached a new height when it was discovered that a flaw in the company's system automatically created Klout profiles for minors who had Facebook accounts. The mistake prompted a reevaluation of the company's position on privacy and a response from Joe Fernandez in the company's blog.

"Like Facebook, Google, and nearly every other company in this space, we are working hard to figure this [privacy issue] out, but will not always get everything right," he wrote. "Recently, we erred in creating profiles for registered users' Facebook friends who had recently interacted with them and did not have private accounts. The public interactions were used to show which Facebook friends that registered user was influencing. While this is OK per Facebook's policy, the data returned to us about friends does not include age information and when we realized that accounts for minors had been created we rolled the changes back.

"We will always be vigilant in working with the platforms (Twitter/Facebook/etc), our legal counsel, and the community to do what's right here. We messed up on this one and are deeply sorry.

"I think it's important to be specific, so here is how Klout thinks about and has always thought about social data:

- Klout analyzes public data to measure a person's influence. The best way to think of this is in relation to how Google analyzes public websites to generate PageRank.
- Klout respects the privacy settings of all the networks it measures. If you have a private account on a social network and you have not explicitly given Klout access to your data it will not be analyzed.
- If you are creating public data but do not want it measured by Klout you can opt-out by going to the privacy page.
- Klout has no interest in understanding the influence of minors. We are working with Facebook and Twitter on this, as well as building our own safeguards to make sure this does not happen."

Although Klout seemingly is adopting and adapting to privacy issues, the vital debate for the entire industry is just beginning. There is an inexorable tension between the intense competitive pressure for these platforms to achieve profitable growth and privacy advocates who want to empower consumers to stop or limit these companies from tracking their online activities.

Today, a relatively small number of insiders truly understand the implications of the social media business model, privacy, and the attention economy. It is not a question of if but a matter of when a privacy meltdown at Facebook, Google, Klout, or some other company will intensify the level of protest and broaden the outcry to a debate at the national level.

But Businesses Still Bite

After all this angst, anger, controversy, lamps, and sheep, you may be thinking, Why am I even reading this book? What could the business benefits possibly be? That's where it gets interesting.

No matter what problems there are involving the meaning, accuracy, viability, and ethics of social scoring, hundreds of companies, including some of the world's biggest brands, are signing up to leverage this new world of citizen influence. Obviously, they see the world differently.

For all the faults, social scoring systems represent a targeted, high-potential, and relatively low-cost way to create buzz about products, services, and brands through powerful niche influencers. That is revolutionary.

Next, let's meet some of the people and companies that are using social scoring to build brand awareness, create cost-effective marketing programs, and sell more lipstick.

CHAPTER 9

The Business Benefits of Social Influence

aprildunford April Dunford
I'm impressed with @klout. A free flight with Virgin America captures your attention in a way $1 off a frappuccino does not
20 Jun 10

Thirty.

That number effectively captures the potential business benefits of Klout for a brand. Joe Fernandez explains: "The biggest thing that happens in a Klout marketing campaign is a lot of content creation. We've found that with every person invited to a campaign, around 30 pieces of content are created.

"So let's say we invite you to a special event. You're going to send a tweet when you first get invited, you're going to take a picture when you get the box of merchandise in the mail, and you might post on Facebook when you start playing with whatever we sent you. You might do a YouTube video of whatever and then maybe a blog post. And then it creates a ripple effect with all of the people you interact with. And now you have authentic conversation driven by passionate, trusted people on a topic that you care about.

"It's like the reverse of a sales funnel. The traditional advertising approach is to hit as many people as possible and a few will funnel out at the bottom. We're hitting a few key influencers at the bottom and letting them tell the story to pass it up through the wider part of the funnel."

The field is so new that statistically valid research is scarce and the brands performing it are understandably hesitant to give it up!

But an insight by the Internet marketing company Eloqua may offer a peek into the power of key influencers' connections. In a limited analysis, Eloqua compared content that was tweeted by individuals with a very high Klout score (70 or above) with a random population of tweets about the same content (five blog posts).

On average, the links embedded in the high-Klout, superconnector tweets were opened and viewed six times more often than were the control group's tweets. In addition, among those who opened the control group link, about 5 percent went on to submit a form requesting more information about the company. In the high-Klout group, the conversion rate was more than double at 12 percent.

Another clue to the impact of superconnectors is revealed by research conducted by Klout that showed that among influencers with a Klout score above 75, their content "lasts" on Twitter (through retweets) up to 70 times longer than that of people with a score between 30 and 70. This finding reinforces the point that those with the most impactful presence on the social web create content that continues to move virally through their networks and beyond. Clearly, this is a radical new way for companies to engage with customers and create marketing interest through the influence they naturally carry in online conversations. And marketers are signing on. More than 3,000 companies are already using Klout's data in some capacity. Before we look at some case studies, let's examine how a marketing program based on Klout scores might work.

The Perks Program

The cornerstone of the Klout commercial program is Perks. Through this initiative, sponsors have the ability to offer Klout users exclusive perk packages that vary with their scores and areas of influence. Here are some examples:

- Audi invited top design, technology, and luxury influencers to test drive the new 2011 Audi A8 at targeted events. A few lucky winners were awarded all-expense-paid weekend trips with the car.
- Universal Pictures invited top entertainment influencers to screen *The Adjustment Bureau* before it was released in theaters.

- Hewlett-Packard offered top film influencers an HP laptop preloaded with the top films from the Cinequest film festival.
- Nike offered first access to a Kobe Bryant short film to users influential in basketball.
- When Disney debuted the movie *Tangled*, it asked Klout to find 500 mothers for exclusive Klout screenings and sent their children a merchandise kit with the film soundtrack, a T-shirt, a stuffed lizard character, and artwork.
- BlackBerry distributed its PlayBook tablet to 100 super-high-scoring tech influencers before the product was released to the public.
- In Las Vegas, the Palms Hotel and Casino is using Klout data to give highly rated guests an upgrade or tickets to Cirque du Soleil. During the annual Consumer Electronics Show, the hotel hosted an event with free food and chair massages for guests with high Klout scores.
- Chevrolet offered free three-day test drives of its 2012 Sonic to influencers with Klout scores over 45 who lived in San Francisco, New York, Atlanta, or Dallas.
- Procter & Gamble offered four sticks of deodorant to 2,500 women whom Klout deemed influential about fitness and entrepreneurship in a promotion linked to the Secret brand's sponsorship of the long-distance swimmer Diana Nyad. Those showered with deodorant samples could also send samples to friends while the 10,000-unit supply lasted. According to *AdAge*, P&G said the campaign generated 5,918 tweets and 15.7 million impressions. "[Klout] has a unique ability to find out who these people are," said Sonny Jandial, associate marketing director at P&G FutureWorks.

One of the most highly successful and well-known campaigns was the introduction of the European music service Spotify to the United States. The company offered free invitations to its service through Klout to any users with a score above 20 regardless of the field in which they were influential. The Spotify deal swept through the Internet buzz machines, brought 250 percent more traffic than average to Klout, and briefly crashed its servers.

Participants who agree to get some benefit from Klout Perks are directed to a Code of Ethics page that describes the expectations this way:

- Klout will never sell or give away your contact info.
- Participating (or not participating) will not change your Klout Score.
- If you accept the offer you are not required to do anything. We do not want to "buy" your tweets. You are receiving the product because you are influential and have authority on topics related to the product. This is a more targeted form of receiving a sample while shopping at the grocery store. You are welcome to tell the world you love the product, you hate the product, or say nothing at all.
- If you decide to talk about the product we will ask you to disclose that you received a sample. Klout suggests using this statement: *I was given a free product or sample because I'm a Klout influencer. I was under no obligation to receive the sample or talk about this company. I get no additional benefits for talking about the product or company.*

In addition to providing free offers to consumers, Shripal Shah, senior vice president, digital, at the Manhattan-based Catalyst Public Relations, explained that Klout Perks provides a turnkey fulfillment solution for brands. "The brand will not interact with the influencers directly, so they create a promotional plan and turn it over to Klout. It might include a link to an offer or even a physical sample. If the program involves sampling or a gift, the product gets sent to Klout's warehouse ahead of the campaign.

"Once you have identified your target audience, Klout will run the promotion from their site or send out as a tweet to those influencers, indicating that they have qualified for a Klout Perk courtesy of brand X, with a link back to an invitation page. That invitation page is cobranded but requires the person to opt in to receive the promotional kit, coupon, or whatever it may be from Klout. At no time does the brand get the data when the user signs up. Klout works hard at that separation, so the only thing the brand can do is look for responses on Twitter, Facebook, or Foursquare to see who is responding to their Perks."

Klout CEO Joe Fernandez said that 80 percent of the companies that have signed up for the Perks program come back for more events and that that has led to an early monetization boon for the young company. "It's been pretty amazing," he said. "We don't do any advertising, but big brands like GE, Pepsi, American Express, and Electronic Arts are contacting us about it. So we've got this sales team who are basically just order takers at this point, because we can't keep up with the demand.

"When we sit down with these brands, the approach is pretty standard right now—connect with somewhere around 100 positive influencers, provide those individuals with some sort of special experience, and track what happens. We know these people are passionate about the topic, we know they're going to be talking about it, and if you create the right scenario, they are going to engage, they are going to create content, and they are going to influence others. The key is letting them tell the story."

Five Key Benefits of Influence Marketing Programs

Shripal Shah has helped connect some of the world's most recognized consumer brands to their customers through Klout programs. He couldn't reveal specific client names but is convinced that tapping into Citizen Influencers is adding a new dimension to those companies' marketing efforts.

Shah is arguably the most experienced Klout marketer in the world. He described five key benefits that he has observed through his campaigns.

1. Authentic Advocacy

"What I think is magic about Klout is you can now find true advocates who already love your brand—perhaps are already writing about your product—and in many cases are having as much, if not more, influence in their niches than mass broadcasters in traditional media," Shah said.

"So now you're sending somebody who Klout has determined is already a fan of this brand a special product, or it could be you're inviting participation in a special event like a movie premiere, or maybe the brand has a new product coming out. Because they are already advocates, you're not asking them to do anything that they're not already doing.

"An analogy I use: I used to work for a pro sports team, and when we were talking to potential sponsors, we would tell them our research has shown a fan of this team is 65 to 85 percent more likely to buy your product when the brand is associated with the franchise. This is how we view these social influencers. They are being viewed as a trusted resource. This is somebody I am following, so what they say day in and day out can likely influence my behavior.

"You may read the newspaper, but that may or may not influence your behavior. But Twitter and Facebook are personal, and people are checking them multiple times a day. So now people you know and love are posting about products in the context of their lives, and that's a powerful connection."

2. Cost-Effective Impressions

"Most media campaigns are measured in terms of the cost per thousand impressions," Shah said. "When the brand is being mentioned in a tweet, in a Facebook post, in a blog post, video, or comment, there's great value to that. We are going out to people who have a huge following and a high degree of influence.

"When you do an ROI analysis, the cost per thousand impressions (CPM) I've seen with Klout is coming in around $1.50 to $3.00. Very reasonable. We have seen some phenomenal ROI because these tweets can lead to blog posts and the blog posts can lead to videos; the videos can then influence traditional media. We see that a lot of traditional media look at social media resources for the next story to cover.

"If you can connect with this kind of influence—and we're talking a campaign that creates anywhere from 20 million to 40 million impressions on Facebook, Twitter, Foursquare—these brands have found a new way to use social media to reach folks and cut through the clutter.

"From the research we've conducted, if you take the investment back to the CPM number, Klout numbers tend to be on par with or better than traditional advertising. But the advantage is that it's not an advertisement; it's more organic. As part of the Klout program, you're not insisting that the influencer writes about your product—it's always voluntary. I like to say it's earned media versus paid media."

3. Fresh Marketing Channel

"In the PR business this type of outreach provides an opportunity to extend the media bureau," Shah explained. "You're complementing your outreach to magazines, newspapers, TV, websites, and blogs. I think there is a certain mommy blogger weariness right now. This gives us an opportunity to get to know a new set of influencers who already like your brand and provide a favorable response, a genuine response. In essence, this is a new marketing channel."

4. Consumer Feedback Loop

"There are well-known firms that will go out and create a focus group or do product sampling for you to get a read of market acceptance," Shah said. "That's in essence how Klout is functioning but with an important difference. When you hire one of these companies, they are the only ones that are distributing your sample.

"Through Klout, the product idea and product review are actually being distributed through other consumers. It's an interesting alternative. It's as if you took a focus group or product sampling group and then asked them to tell their friends what they thought. We can then monitor that conversation and learn from it.

"If I were working with a product sampling group, I would be shipping, say, 500 or 5,000 pieces of a product and then try to understand who liked it, who didn't, and why. You will get a lot more data and demographic information from that method. Klout offers another data point. You can see who is tweeting about your product and who their followers are, and you can begin creating these social profiles of who likes your product. So if you look at those personas as a new kind of focus group, you can begin to build on that feedback. It is an influencer group you could, in theory, go back to in six months with the next product offering."

5. Brand Buffer

Shah also said that Klout adds unique value by acting as an intermediary between consumers and brands.

"Most consumers don't want the brands contacting them directly on Twitter or Facebook," he explained. "It's like spam e-mail: You don't want to be inundated with messages about things that you may or may not want. Just because I buy their brand every week doesn't mean I want their weekly e-mail or Facebook updates. So Klout coming in as an intermediary provides some sense of privacy. I think that fact provides some of the most interesting value that I've seen from these programs."

"Klout is definitely gaining traction with important brands," Shah said. "We are seeing that brands that we've introduced Klout to are eager to use it again. Look at Disney. Not one of my clients, but they used Klout successfully with their *Tangled* movie, so when they came out with a new Winnie the Pooh movie, there was a Winnie the Pooh Klout campaign. Disney is a big, powerful brand and was an early adopter of Klout, so are people going to dismiss them as a young pup or a fly by the seat of your pants type of company?

"I think that's the litmus test for success. Are brands coming back? Pepsi and Audi have done programs multiple times and are now starting to expand the use of Klout influencers into other areas like a Facebook campaign. Big brands I am working with are seeing similar type of results and are signing up for more."

Case Studies: Klout at Work

Let's take a look at a few real case studies that illustrate the variety of ways large and small businesses are beginning to use social scoring results to drive buzz, solve problems, connect to customers, and create new commercial opportunities.

Turner Broadcasting: New Product Introduction

Fergus Thomas, director of interactive and social media at Atlanta's Turner Broadcasting System (TBS), is a marketing veteran who fully realizes the potential of social media marketing. Perhaps because he is a former brand manager for Coke Zero, his eyes were opened to the way his target demographic of young males was interacting with media in radically new ways.

"I started realizing the way we were connecting and talking with consumers was fundamentally changing," he said. "Our TV ads were not nearly as effective. Enormous amounts of time were being spent on Facebook and social networking sites, so we needed to experiment in this area too, primarily with online games. One game generated a million consumer interactions a day with no media spend. Before that, we had been focused on traditional sports marketing, but that opened my eyes a bit."

Thomas was brought over to TBS to create a center of excellence for social media. "After my experience at Coke, I immediately recognized the tremendous opportunity to work with a television network. I mean, if you're going to be working with social media, it's not bad to be in a company where the entire business is predicated on generating great content."

One of the first things Thomas did was organize and staff a department aimed at external consumer engagement. "The way we're looking at social [media] more and more is that we're trying to drive mass-scale brand endorsements," he said, "trying to get this idea of social ubiquity. So how do we activate consumers and have them engage with our brands, and how do we get them to spread the message to their friends?"

TBS connected to Klout in a roundabout way. The network had just landed one of TV's biggest stars, Conan O'Brien, and had inherited a fan base of rabid loyalists. It was the biggest program launch in the network's history and a perfect test case to see if the social web could be used to activate and involve the loco Team Coco.

"Initially, we were making the rounds to visit Facebook and Twitter about that time, and Klout was in the basement of the Twitter building, and they were like 'Hey, you're going to be out here, you should drop by,' and we did. It was a wreck of an office. Stuff everywhere. I didn't even have a chair to sit on, so it was . . . different. You could tell these guys had been living there for a couple of days straight, so they had to clear some papers to give us a place to sit. But it was helpful for me to see that dedication and passion.

"They were just starting out, but they were already doing some really interesting work. We got into some discussions about possibly mining this social data and beginning to tie together influence and actions—not just comments but *action* on those comments. Whether it's a retweet or somebody opening a link, we could observe people reacting to conversations by specific topics. As a network, we could leverage this and prove out our models because we had a built-in crowd who was (a) influential and (b) interested in our particular topic.

"We tried our first full Klout Perks campaign a few months later to support a show called *Southland*," Thomas continued. "It was another show we saved from being discontinued off the networks. The fan base was relatively small, but we got impressive results for the amount of money and time and energy we spent on the Klout campaign.

"We looked primarily at impressions, realizing that with that number there's always a bit of a BS factor to determine what an impression is worth. But one of the benefits of Klout is that they can break down these impressions and help you get to a real number, something distilled down to the actual active and engaged audience.

"We only reached out to about 300 people, who generated thousands of tweets and comments, but more important, 95 percent of them were really positive online conversations about the show. We got tweets from people saying, 'I got my perk and will be watching the show' and 'The show is awesome . . . you need to watch this,' and that is exactly what we were looking for.

"At the end of the day, we ended up with something like 3 million impressions. You start to think, Wow. I mean, it was just an experiment, but it showed the potential of this idea to find and engage with the people who care about you.

"Our traditional approach would be to send out press packages and early screenings to the press, critics, *TV Guide*, and others who were historically influential because they controlled a media outlet. So now we're taking this content and putting it in the hands of normal people who would probably be more likely to amplify the message. That went so well that within a few months we did four more campaigns with similar results."

Thomas and his team then attempted a different marketing approach with a new show they were launching. "We were going to launch a new program called *Falling Skies*, a sci-fi program produced by Steven Spielberg, and we decided to take a different approach. We had completed some research that showed that consistency in content drives the Facebook algorithm. If your fans interact with one post, they are more and more likely to interact with the next post, and the next post. We've seen accounts where we stopped posting and then when we start posting again, it takes people a long time to catch back up and start connecting again. Our fans look for consistency and reward consistency.

"So with *Falling Skies* we thought about this lesson about consistency. Wouldn't engaging with them more consistently drive the same behavior we observed on Facebook? It seemed logical.

"We essentially set up a 10-week campaign and invited 600 influencers. They received something from Klout each week that revealed some inside secret, a digital experience, about the upcoming episode. So they had an insight into the story before anybody else. Some weeks we actually sent them a physical gift or clue, but it was all geared toward driving the mystery and the conversation.

"We put a lot of thought and effort into the perks the participants received each week. The last thing you want to do with these people is send them something crappy. They will just as easily tweet about how crappy you and your free gift are. I had to continually have these conversations with marketing people who just wanted to give out old DVDs or jackets. So I asked them, 'If I gave this to you, would you go home and tell anybody about it? Would you tell your friends or call up your mom and say, "Hey I got a free DVD today"?' That's the lens we have to have. . . . What can we give them that they will go home and call up their friends and say, 'You won't believe what I just got!' If you want to inspire an influencer, you can't just send them the same coupon everybody else gets. That defeats the purpose.

"We also had Klout create a 'leader board,' and at the end of the season, the person who had the highest Klout score on the topic of

Falling Skies was awarded a walk-on role at the beginning of season two.

"This was an amazingly successful campaign. Not only did we experience a tenfold increase in the amount of conversation we saw compared to other shows, the rate of the conversation increased from week to week, which totally took us by surprise. For a normal show, Twitter conversations will show a huge spike at the premiere; it falls off the next day, and you get a gradual decline until the big spike again at the finale.

"That's not what happened this time. Because the Klout conversations had their own hashtag, we were able to break that out from organic conversations. At the beginning, we saw that normal spike. Kind of what I expected. About 90 percent of the total conversations were organic, and 10 percent were driven by Klout. We sat back and expected to see the normal lull in the following weeks, but the exact opposite happened! As the season continued, the amount of Klout conversations got bigger and bigger each week. It was bizarre. The volume of the conversation became so great that I actually saw a consumer electronics company start to tweet with our hashtag just to become part of our Twitter conversation!

"By the end of the campaign we saw that this small group of Klout influencers was driving about 60 percent of this huge conversation out there. The Klout influencers had formed a community around the show."

"You would expect that with this special prize people might game the conversation by simply repeating the hashtag over and over," Thomas said. "But we did an analysis and didn't really see that. The conversation was normal stuff about the characters and why the aliens were here. So it was really impressive to see they got that involved with it. They were even asking us for more contests when this first season ended. That kind of response was unprecedented. So now it's up to us to find ways to keep these people engaged, and that's where we're at right now."

What is the potential return of a program like this? An analysis conducted by NM Incite and Nielsen looked at the correlation between online buzz and television ratings and found a statistically significant relationship throughout a TV show's season among all age groups. A 14 percent increase in buzz translates to an increase of a full point in ratings. TBS and other television content providers are finding that creating and nurturing online buzz results in measurable gains in ratings and advertising revenue.

Working Social Proof into a Traditional Marketing Campaign

Social proof seems to be having a marketable value for businesses, too. The start-up Addoway is an online marketplace that matches buyers with trustworthy friends and merchants by integrating information from Facebook and other online sources. The company experimented by adding seller Klout scores to its listings and found that it increased the likelihood of a sale by 500 percent.

CEO Fredrick Nijm, quoted by ecommerceBytes.com, said that Klout's attempt to measure a user's true reach in her social networking circle seems to resonate with his customers. "Klout scores can make buyers feel more comfortable buying from strangers," he said. "The scores give buyers a glimpse of how long sellers have been online and how active they are." Nijm is convinced that Klout scores can positively influence shoppers when they are evaluating sellers who are unknown to them.

Audi: Building Advocates Outside the Traditional Fan Base

The German auto manufacturer Audi has been at the forefront of social scoring experimentation. An early trial was aimed at attracting noncore auto fans to start talking about Audi's high-tech products in diverse online communities.

Audi asked Klout to identify tech writers, photography nuts, and others who would appreciate the craftsmanship and beauty of its automobiles. They invited those targeted influencers to exclusive Klout-only events in Los Angeles and San Francisco that showcased the cars and offered weekend test drives.

Paul Meyers is a digital marketing manager with M80, the firm that managed the social media project for Audi. "When Audi introduced its flagship A8 sedan, we decided to test the Klout program," he said. "It might not seem that a luxury car like that is necessarily going to show up in the social space, but Audi's end goal wasn't really ROI. They wanted to get this car into the hands of people with influence around technology, much as they do with the traditional trade press. We measured success by showing how many mentions, reach among influencers, and exactly what were they saying, much like a traditional PR campaign.

"Our goal was to nurture new brand advocates in the social space. An example would be a guy named Jim Alden, who was identified as a key influencer by Klout. We reached out to him, and he came to Los Angeles to see the car, and we set him up with a short drive: three days. He received the same treatment that was usually reserved for the elite trade press. And Jim created a lot of great content based on that experience. There's no way that we could have pinpointed Mr. Alden as somebody who would be interested in the Audi brand, and he is. In fact, I still keep in contact with him on a personal level. He loves cars and he loves technology, so he's like our ideal fan. In that regard, it was kind of cool to see what Klout can do on that level. Our number one goal was exposure, and we think that a Klout score shows that people are using social media in an effective way."

"Noah Kravitz was another new nontraditional fan who came to us through Klout," said Meyers. "He was at the San Francisco event, and he posted an amazing video about the car for his blog, a site that covers gadgets and gear but wouldn't normally cover a new car. He highlighted the fact that the A8 was one of the first cars that had Wi-Fi capability as an option. That type of content is a direct hit to the type of community we were trying to get to talk about the car."

The Audi campaign also utilized new applications that allowed the company to filter its attention and interact with millions of engaged Facebook fans by using Klout-derived influence scores. The brand is able to show content that varies with users' Klout scores.

"We identified Klout as a skilled partner to help us recognize and identify our Facebook fans with followings and influence," said Doug Clark, general manager, social media & customer engagement, at Audi of America. "We currently have over 3.5 million fans on Facebook, and we see this as a great tool to help manage and work more directly with our fan base."

Influencers and Nonprofit Organizations

In the world of nonprofit fund-raising, the competition for donor dollars is every bit as fierce and strategic as the daily battles among corporate giants. Identifying and connecting with high-potential donors is a complex task.

The Helen Brown Group is one of the world's leading consulting practices in the cottage industry of donor research. The founder of this Boston-based company thinks that social scoring systems have the potential to be integrated into this difficult field.

"Privacy is the ultimate concern with anything we do," said Helen Brown. "Our reputation depends on much more than just following the law. Sensitivity and compassion are important elements to consider when approaching people to donate to a cause. It's not just about data. Your heart has to be engaged in the process, too."

For that reason, many nonprofits have been cautious when it comes to integrating social media platforms into donor research efforts. "You never want to be in a position of stalking people," Brown said. "There is a creepiness factor there that probably will never go away.

"However, I do see how Klout could be a useful buffer between the personal information being shared on the web and the legitimate interests of a nonprofit agency. Since potential donors are signing up for Klout and freely offering their information to this company, this might be a way to match the personal interests of potential donors with charitable causes they would love.

"I also think that nonprofits could pay attention to prospects' Klout scores and the number of followers a prospect has to help decide who to approach to serve on charitable boards. The more connections (and therefore influence) someone has in society, the more they can be a potent connector to funding sources, business acumen, and other capacity-building resources."

Depaul UK, a youth homelessness charity, partnered with PeerIndex and the advertising agency Publicis to put this idea to the test. The partnership used PeerIndex analytics to target key social media influencers to get people talking about iHobo, a smartphone application aimed at increasing awareness about homelessness among a younger, affluent audience.

Applying Influence in the Moment

LocalResponse is a start-up that gives businesses access to a dashboard that shows who and where all of their customers are. Through Twitter, businesses can send public replies to thank them for their patronage or even offer a coupon. LocalResponse will also sort customers by their level of local influence as measured by Klout or by how many times a mention of their designated products appears in a person's news feed.

In its first six months, a private beta campaign featuring 2,000 companies had spectacular success. Targeted messages sent through LocalResponse had a 60 percent click-through rate.

Another company working on applying influence marketing at a hyper-local level is LoClout, which is building a database of users generated by their reach and engagement through social media platforms within a geographic radius. The company is scouring raw social media traffic data, popular user lists, bookmarks, and "elite" memberships in Yelp, Foursquare, and other networks to develop influence scores based on local interactions.

Klout and an Advertising Agency

Dane Hartzell, chief digital strategist for Minneapolis-based Bolin Marketing, saw the possibilities of Klout almost from the beginning.

"I started using Klout for business right away, trying to build groups of consumers or influencers based on who they are or where they might have influence," he said. "We are currently working through this ranking of key influencers for each of our customer brands. This is going to help us become a lot more targeted, effective, and efficient. For example, sometimes we might be sending out a pretty elaborate kit for sampling and we can't afford to send it to everybody in the network, so we start at the top based on how we've tiered them with regard to influence. So we were really excited when Klout came along because it helped us to build these influence models."

"Before we had Klout, we were kind of doing a lot of this influence assessment manually," he said. "We started working with blogger networks long ago and worked with a group of about 300 bloggers who had a readership that matched the demographics of the product or service we were working with. We had developed a pretty large database and started ranking based on things like traffic and comments and other criteria like pageviews, inbound links that come to them, etc. But we realized that those aren't the only channels that people use nowadays. There are many, many other influencers out there in many areas other than blogs. So Klout fills a need to help us find those folks."

"We use Klout to help us serve niche industries," Hartzell said. "For example, we are working on a project for an interior design client, and there are only a handful of bloggers who have any major reach, but there are a lot of people talking about interior design on social networks. We've used Klout as the entry point to see who has influence, what they're talking about, and who has influence on them."

Integration with Traditional Coupon Incentive Programs

Paul Saarinen, director of digital insights and culture for Bolin Marketing, said that the firm is integrating traditional marketing efforts, social media monitoring activities, and Klout influencer data to create new customer value.

"We're working on a program for a major consumer packaged goods company and are actively monitoring for complaints about their competition," he said. "Then we can reach out to those people who have complained about a bad experience with any competitor's brand, segment them by Klout score, and offer them a coupon for our product. And by the way, the higher the Klout score, the higher the coupon value they receive.

"We are working with some other CPG [consumer packaged goods] brands that use coupons, and we are helping them rethink their traditional coupon strategy. Rather than sending out 46 million of them in a newspaper insert, we're trying to get more and more of that to be online. At the moment it might not have the scale of other channels, depending on the demographic, but it has lots of other benefits like much more data, much more opportunity for these things to be passed along, much more organic advocacy. We call it a 'competitive targeting program': using Klout scores to help find the people who can best help us in the marketplace."

Identifying and Nurturing B2B Thought Leadership

The Bolin Agency is using Klout scores in an interesting B2B application. By mashing up sentiment analysis[1] technology with influence scores, they are finding a new way to drive a brand awareness program for a major B2B customer.

"We have a project that is using influence scores for a leading global logistics supply provider," said Hartzell. "They are actually the largest company like this in the world, but they don't have the brand recognition of some of their competitors. We did a sentiment analysis and found that most people talking about our customer were identifying it as a broker for trucks and containers. That is really inconsistent with its core business now. They've evolved to be a logistics solutions company, but nobody is thinking of them this way.

"Through our analysis, we were able to show them this discrepancy, and it was a real wake-up call for senior management. So we put this series of programs together to identify the influencers in their category like the VP of logistics at Coca-Cola, an editor from a trade publication, or even an entire industry LinkedIn Group and then rank those influencers by Klout score. Now we had a starting

---

1. A sentiment analysis in this context refers to software and human analysis that determines the attitude of a writer or group of writers on the social web. Sophisticated programs can assess millions of pieces of social media content to see high-level trends and hot spots.

point for an outreach program to try to establish thought leadership from the customer.

"Klout can be used as one way to come up with a tiered list of decision makers that you want to work with, prioritize an editorial calendar, and learn about who is influencing the influencer."

Prioritizing Customer Service Responses

Naveen Krishnamurthy, president/CEO of RIVA Solutions, Inc., has been experimenting with integrating influence scores into the customer service experience.

"Being aware of consumer challenges appearing in social media is only a small part of managing online sentiment," he said. "Action is key. Our team uses sentiment analysis software to identify complaints but then analyze and rank each one according to an influencer report card and craft a rapid response. By using Klout, we can try to assure our customers that comments which could have the most potential negative impact are handled first.

"We've learned that it costs more if the first response is not effective because consumers will not only complain again, they are also likely to share their unhappy experiences with prospective consumers throughout the web. Done well, we can often convert negative sentiment into positive commentary about the brand."

Influence Marketing and the Pass-Along Strategy

Plum District is a start-up aimed at connecting the best daily deals and coupons with moms around the United States. The model depends on support from the moms themselves and widespread adoption, since they are also contributing the best deals they can find in their cities.

The experience of integrated marketing and social commerce director Melissa Shymko shows that success with influence marketing can depend on experimentation and iteration. They knew about Klout because they are neighbors in the same building in San Francisco.

"Klout approached us and offered their services, and we were really excited and intrigued because we know how influential and engaged moms are on the web," Shymko said. "We were eager to try something out with Klout and see if we could reach them with a demonstration of our product."

Plum District decided to implement a pass-along strategy in which somebody who receives a Klout Perk has the ability to give a similar gift to his friends; this is an opportunity to extend the reach of the program far beyond Klout influencers to a new network of superconnectors.

In the first experiment, the company sent a $50 certificate good for shopping on the Plum District website, with pass-along friends receiving a $25 certificate.

"We didn't reach our cap-out target on this first round," she said. "The initial redemption rate was excellent: around 50 percent participation, and 90 percent of these new customers had never heard of Plum District before. Even more significant, 100 percent of the new customers made a second purchase from our site within 90 days of using the Klout Perk. So certainly Klout had been able to identify a very qualified demographic for us: moms who were out there talking about deals, savings, and how to make it on a budget. Those are exactly the kind of people we're interested in reaching.

"However, the viral aspect of the program didn't really take off like we thought it would. There was a lot of content generation about the promotion, but the $25 certificates were not passed along extensively. Our leading theory was that moms who received the first certificate thought that if they passed along the certificate offer, maybe they would be replaced and not receive the Klout deals in the future. But we don't know for sure. We needed to keep experimenting."

"So in our second trial," Shymko continued, "we changed three things: The pass-along coupon was the same value as the original one, we lowered the value of all the coupons to $10, and we created an incentive program so that those who had the most successful pass-alongs could be eligible for other rewards like a free iPad 2.

"Our conversion rate in this round dropped from 50 percent to just 10 percent, probably due to the lower value of the certificate. These women bloggers are flooded with opportunities all the time. They are in sample and discount overload! So maybe the $10 was not enough to get their attention like the $50 award did.

"However, the pass-along aspect was much more successful. We generated four times more conversions via pass-along. So the results were mixed. I did like the organic feel of the campaign compared to buying ads: If you like us, talk about us and share with your friends.

"The results of the trials weren't conclusive, but we learned enough that I would definitely do it again. Next time I think we will take more risk with the value of the award and the number of people we are trying to reach. I don't lose anything if people don't come to the site to use the code, so the cost and risk is low to continue experimenting."

Social Scoring and Crisis Management

David Rosen, a director in the corporate practice at the global PR firm Burson-Marsteller, uses social scoring in a number of public relations applications, but none is as important as crisis management.

In 2011, a blogger posted that one of the firm's clients might go bankrupt, but the analysis was based on inaccurate financial data. If the information spread, it could create a PR nightmare and affect the company's stock.

Burson-Marsteller had to decide quickly what action to recommend to its client.

"We saw that the handful of tweeters who picked up the post had very low Klout scores," Rosen said. "Based on this, we concluded that it was unlikely that the news would spread enough to have an impact and advised the client to wait and watch. If a low number of tweeters with large scores—or a large number of tweeters with low scores—retweeted the story, then aggressive action would have been required. But at that moment, the combination of low Klout and knowing that the client's institutional investors were well educated on the company's balance sheet meant that restraint was the best action. We ended up being right, and the meme quickly died.

"At a time when news can spread in the blink of an eye, we have found Klout to be a useful shorthand indicator when we need to make a decision quickly."

Influence Marketing Best Practices

Throughout these case studies a few themes emerge as best practices. If you're thinking about trying Klout, PeerIndex, or any of the other social scoring platforms coming on the scene, here are a few things to keep in mind:

- *Do you have a conversational brand?* This type of marketing will work only if your target audience is engaging with your brand on the social web. If you're in the business of selling ball bearings to automotive manufacturers, there are probably better ways to spend your marketing budget.

- *Have a strategy.* Don't expect social scoring companies to develop a marketing strategy. All the success stories in this book were based on first having the research and customer insight to know that investing in an influencer campaign was a good bet. The goals of your strategy should be specific and measurable.
- *Relevance.* You can't just reach out to an influencer because she has a large audience and you'd like her to talk about your brand. You have to ensure that the product is pertinent to each individual and her audience. Is there a natural group of influencers you can identify regardless of the size of the audience?
- *Let your partner do the heavy lifting.* As Shripal Shah pointed out, it is actually an advantage to have the brand one step removed from the process. You will get a higher response rate when the message comes from an intermediary. Influencers are more likely to trust the intermediary with their information.
- *Keep it real.* Influencers are trusted because they share their genuine opinions, both good and bad. Ensuring the authenticity of the engagement is a key to its success. It's likely that some of the engagement is going to be negative because it's a human interaction. Manage expectations and expect some negativity.
- *Keep it legal.* In 2010, the U.S. Federal Trade Commission (FTC) issued guidelines stating that bloggers must reveal when they are receiving compensation or free merchandise related to something they are writing about. Broadly interpreted, a tweet could be seen as the equivalent of a blog post.
- *Don't get too specific.* The broader your potential audience is, the more likely you are to find influencers who love you. If you are working for a company selling handbags, you'll probably have more success finding people talking about fashion than about purses. If you are marketing a new camera, technology and gadget influencers are probably as likely to ignite an epidemic about your brand as are people tweeting about photography, and there are more of the former. Remember that topical influence is more important than somebody's overall score.
- *Go local.* The major platforms such as PeerIndex and Klout have some ability to find influencers by geographic area. Don't overlook this opportunity.

- *Pay attention to your perk.* Fergus Thomas characterized this really well in the TBS case study. Give your influencers something to talk about! The higher the "wow" factor of a perk, the more amplification and impressions you will probably receive. Examples of successful perks include access codes to valuable digital content, exclusive events, and free merchandise.
- *Make it shareable.* Create a specific hashtag for your promotion. If you have a live event, make sure there is reliable free Wi-Fi service. Provide easily shareable digital content. Encourage influencers to bring guests or invite others to your promotion; they'll share too.

Keeping It Legal

Though all the best practices discussed above are important, I want to give extra attention to the idea of keeping a project legal before we close the chapter. As was mentioned, in 2010, the FTC passed a regulation requiring bloggers and social media agents to make a disclosure when writing about products they've gotten for free. Although a status update may be 140 characters or less, it is placed under the same disclosure guidelines as a full-length blog; this has created a stir about what amount of disclosure is practical and possible in a microblogging format.

Klout sends every person involved in its influence programs a link to a disclosure page that provides recommended disclosure statements. Telling influencers to make a disclosure, however, isn't the same as making sure they actually do it. Klout's disclaimer may shield it from liability, but brand partners could potentially be legally exposed if they don't act to verify that disclosures are really being made.

Glen Gilmore, an attorney and founder of Gilmore Business Network, said: "Brands using Klout must also participate in both the instruction of the duty to disclose and the monitoring of sponsored bloggers for a disclosure of the perk they have received when blogging/tweeting about the brand. It would seem to me that an advertiser could not simply delegate to a vendor its obligations under the guidelines. At the same time, the guidelines do not specify the extent or nature of the monitoring program that must be in place, though commentary in FTC settlements suggests that random sampling of sponsored bloggers may suffice."

With new technologies and platforms constantly being introduced and evolving, FTC regulations will continue to play a role.
How these regulations develop over time will inevitably affect how
companies are able to utilize the perk programs of Klout and other
social scoring sites.

Now that you've seen how many of the world's most important
brands are willing to dangle goodies in front of influencers for a
tweet or two, you might be wondering how you can get a piece of the
action. How can you become part of the Twitterati, the Klout elite,
a leader in the new Citizen Influencer movement?

Let's find out.

CHAPTER 10

How to Increase Your Klout Score

mayhemstudios Calvin Lee
@TheLittleWendy: Klout score depends on engagement, retweets, other RT'ing U. Who your followers connected to, how influential they are.
15 hours ago

Perhaps this is the moment you've been waiting for: real advice on improving your Klout or PeerIndex score to enter the ranks of Citizen Influencers. But first you're going to have to deal with an unpleasant fact: Between the time you read this book's Introduction and the time you have reached this chapter, Klout's algorithm for measuring influence has probably changed. Even if I had access to the secret recipe, it would be out of date, and tomorrow it would be out of date—ever so slightly—again.

But never fear. There are definitely some universal truths we can learn from Klout and leading academics in the field of influence that can provide guidance for optimizing our personal brands, our web presence, and, yes, our Klout scores.

Can these tactics really work? In this chapter we'll get a firsthand look from technology expert Neelu Modali, who used the concepts presented here to increase his Klout score by 30 points in 45 days. Yes, it works.

Let's start with an overview of how Klout processes these massive amounts of data so that we can understand how it sees the world.

Measuring a Sliver of Influence

The Merriam-Webster dictionary defines influence as "the power or capacity of causing an effect in indirect or intangible ways." Easy enough. But despite decades of research and the formulation of theories of influence in sociology, marketing, psychology, and political science, there has been no tangible way to measure this force rapidly, inexpensively, and across a broad population. Until now.

Simply put, Klout's complex mathematical models are used in an attempt to determine just one thing: your ability to produce an effect, an online reaction, in a topical niche. A Klout score is a proxy for how well you can move your content—ideas, opinions, reviews, videos, thoughts, and the like—to other people in a way that makes them react. The extent to which the people who move your content are also influencers helps drive a higher influence score.

Klout doesn't measure all personal influence and never will. But it measures one important sliver of influencer activity increasingly well, with statistical predictability, and that is a huge step toward understanding networks and the movement of ideas in our society.

Think of it this way. As an extreme example, you would be regarded as very influential in the offline world if you created a report that was circulated to your CEO or a head of state, compared with me, since I consider myself lucky to get a timely response from my local cable company. So, you are naturally more influential if your content can influence the influencers. Make sense? That's what Klout is about.

The quality of your friends and followers, how much you participate, and the likelihood of people spreading your information are among the most important variables in the equation.

Klout also places you on something called the influence matrix, which is made up of 16 classifications. You might be a specialist (someone whose content is focused on a specific topic or industry) or a curator (like Calvin Lee, who filters massive amounts of content and gleans nuggets of information from it). Or you might be an activist, a networker, a dabbler, a taste maker, a thought leader, a pundit, or a celebrity. A celebrity is considered the highest level of influencer in the Klout universe.

Each registered user on Klout is assigned "topics" of influence, based on a semantic analysis of their content, which is also prioritized by how actively your network reacts to the content. As we have already seen, Klout is far from a perfect system. At various times I have been deemed to be an influencer in "Sesame Street" and "gold," but presumably the categorization system will be getting better. It will have to because this is an absolutely key component of Klout's value proposition to its customers as brands seek to connect with the right word-of-mouth influencers.

Actual Klout scores are not calculated like grades on a pass or fail basis. Each individual's score is a single number based on three broad aspects of online influence across many social media platforms such as Facebook, LinkedIn, YouTube, blogs, and Twitter. Those categories are true reach, amplification probability, and network influence.

- The *true reach* component tries to determine whether your audience is really engaged with you or whether you are just broadcasting to a bunch of spam accounts. Remarkably, Klout attempts to calculate influence for each individual relationship in your network, taking into account factors such as whether an individual has shared or acted on your content and the likelihood that he or she saw it. Some of the factors in this measurement include your number of followers/friends, mutual follows, retweets, unique comments, likes and tweets, follower/follow ratio, number of mentions, and Twitter lists you are on, among others.

- *Amplification probability* is the likelihood that your content will be acted on. This is the action that is being measured. For example, how often do your messages get shared or spark a conversation? Does your content get spread to other influencers, and do they react? The ability to create content that compels others to respond and high-velocity content that spreads into networks beyond your own are key components of online influence. A few of the amplification factors in the Klout score include number (and percentage) of unique individuals sharing your content, number of your messages that are shared, Facebook likes/comments per post, and inbound messages versus outbound messages.

- *Network influence* is a calculation of your level of power over your engaged audience. Engagement is measured on the basis of actions such as retweets, @messages, follows, lists, comments, and likes.[1] Each time a person performs one of these actions, it is a testament to the authority and quality of your

---

1. All of this terminology is covered in Appendix A.

content. Capturing the attention of influencers is not an easy task, and those who are able to do so are typically creating, or sometimes curating, exceptional content. The network portion of the Klout score considers the influence of the people who interact, follow, and list you. This score is a little incestuous, since the influence of your followers is also determined by Klout.

Other systems, such as PeerIndex and Kred, use similar standards, tweaking details or displaying the data in different ways, but every measure is still assessing an individual's ability to move content through an engaged online network.

There are nuances to these calculations for every social network. For example, people relate to each other differently on YouTube than they do on Facebook or on Twitter versus LinkedIn. Klout builds algorithms from the ground up for every network. There are even considerations for regions and culture. For example, the way people in Indonesia use Twitter may look like spam in other cultures. Subtle shifts in the formulas account for these differences as they are discovered.

How Klout Determines Your Score

Although we don't have access to Klout's secret sauce, we have seen academic research from this field that is probably an accurate indicator of what Klout is using to determine your score. One of the most important published works is a 2011 technical paper called "Influence and Passivity in Social Media" by Daniel Romero, Wojciech Goluba, Sitaram Asur, and Bernardo Huberman.

In this study, the researchers defined influence narrowly, but also in a highly measurable, Klout-like way: Can people move other people to take action and click on a link? They explained their approach: "Given this widespread generation and consumption of content, it is natural to target one's messages to highly connected people who will propagate them further in the social network. This is particularly the case in Twitter, which is one of the fastest growing social networks on the Internet, and thus the focus of advertising companies and celebrities eager to exploit this vast new medium."

"As a result," the study continues, "ideas, opinions, and products compete with all other content for the scarce attention of the user community. In spite of the seemingly chaotic fashion with which all these interactions take place, certain topics manage to get an inordinate amount of attention, thus bubbling to the top in terms of popularity and contributing to new trends and to the public agenda of the community. How this happens in a world where crowdsourcing dominates is still an unresolved problem, but there is considerable consensus on the fact that two aspects of information transmission seem to be important in determining which content receives inordinate amounts of attention."

The study found that the first aspect is the popularity and status of members of the social networks as measured by the level of attention they receive in the form of followers who create links to their accounts to automatically receive the content they generate. The second aspect is the influence these individuals wield, which is determined by the actual propagation (or movement) of their content through the network. This influence is determined by many factors, such as the novelty and resonance of their messages with their followers and the quality and frequency of the content they generate.

"Equally important is the passivity of members of the network which provides a barrier to propagation that is often hard to overcome," the study states. "Thus *gaining knowledge of the identity of influential and least passive people in a network can be extremely useful* [italics added] from the perspectives of viral marketing, propagating one's point of view, as well as setting which topics dominate the public." By analyzing millions of tweets and studying who clicked on what links over time, the researchers could understand which Twitter users were getting the most attention and develop a model to predict that level of influence over time.

The researchers concluded that for individuals to become influential they must not only obtain attention and thus become popular but also overcome user resistance; as we have seen, most people on Twitter do not have a tendency to pass on information. Social media popularity (in terms of number of followers) does not necessarily equate to influence. And, there can be no influence without content that was interesting enough to be moved from person to person, engaging the audience along its path.

This idea was also the centerpiece of research conducted by University of Pennsylvania (Wharton School) marketing professors Raghuram Iyengar and Christophe Van den Bulte. Their study showed that the spread of a product by word of mouth is dependent on "weak links" who are more likely to disseminate information.

The researchers tracked the behavior of physicians in three cities— San Francisco, Los Angeles, and New York—looking specifically at

how quickly they started prescribing a new drug to treat a potentially lethal disease. They surveyed those physicians and identified
a group of "self-reported opinion leaders": doctors who reported
themselves as being well-connected, influential members of the
community. They also identified a second group they called "sociometric leaders": the most influential and well-respected physicians in
the community, based on how often they were mentioned by their
peers.

The study showed that the two measures of opinion leadership
did not overlap in terms of influence. It turns out that asking people
how important they are is not the best measure of how important
they really are!

For example, a key igniter, identified as Physician 184, didn't fit
the description of an individual who marketers thought would be the
most effective promoter of their product: an outgoing, high-profile
doctor whose name often pops up on research papers or on conference speaker lists. He was self-effacing—the opposite of a rock
star—but widely known in the local community and more likely to
network and have the ear of his colleagues. These sociometric leaders were more effective influencers than were the best-known people
in their field, causing marketers to rethink their approach to word-
of-mouth marketing.

The researchers speculate that self-reported "opinion leaders" are
less interested in what others are doing and less affected by those
around them.

The Three Steps to Improving Your Klout Score

Let's get into the guts of the issue. How do we take what we have
learned so far about online influence and apply it in practical ways
to improve a Klout score? There are three steps:

1. Build a relevant network.
2. Have a strategy to provide compelling content.
3. Systematically engage influencers who are most willing (or
   least passive) to distribute your content virally.

Step 1: Build a Relevant Network
One of the things we've learned on this journey is that building a
power base on the Internet requires two foundational elements: a

content strategy and a network strategy. In extreme cases in which content goes viral, it may be possible to attain influence without building a network, but it is never possible to attain online influence without creating content.

An example of this is Rebecca Black or any number of YouTube stars who stumbled upon success, either famously or infamously. The teenage singer had no significant online network, but she did have content: a music video that most decried as, well, not very good. But her commitment and innocence captured the attention of legitimate superstars such as Katy Perry and Lady Gaga, who became her defenders. With the validation of those superstar networks, Rebecca became an overnight sensation, appearing on talk shows, in music videos, and in magazines around the world.

I hate to disappoint you, but this probably isn't going to happen to you. I don't think you and I can count on Lady Gaga to help support our influence strategy. Like the other 99.99 percent who aren't going to have a viral music video that lands them on Letterman, we've got to work at it.

There are many books, blog posts, and other resources dedicated to teaching you how to build an engaged personal network. Here are a few tips:

- The social web is like a chemistry experiment. You want to create some sort of personal or business benefit, which is the chemical reaction. To get there, the more molecules you have in your test tube (people in your audience), the better the chances are that they will collide. And they probably won't collide at all without a catalyst, which is the content. So, in a way, numbers do matter. It's just like sales. You have to make a lot of cold calls to get leads, and you have to have a lot of leads to close a sale.
- The quality and nature of the connections are paramount. You want to find people who have an affinity for you and what you do. You need to find targeted, relevant connections who are going to be interested in you and your content. The actual size of your network is less important as long as the people around you are reacting to you. Having more people follow you than you follow on Twitter will also improve your score.
- Keep your house clean. Since part of Klout's algorithm reflects the amount of audience engagement, you are not

going to benefit from collecting a lot of friends and followers that are empty accounts and never interact. There are dozens of third-party applications that can help you weed out inactive connections. It is important to realize that people who send only links 100 percent of the time are not helping your Klout score because they can't be influenced into acting. Unless they are moving your content or are presenting exceedingly good information, you might rethink their place in your tribe if they're not creating value in some other way.

A common question about the impact of the number of social media platforms on your Klout score is: Does being in many different social networks help you or hurt you? Klout gives more weight to your primary channels, where you are most influential, and then adds in the other platforms that you might be involved in to a lesser degree.

"As far as somebody being on 3 social networks versus 50, we're network agnostic," said Joe Fernandez of Klout. "So if you're just on Yelp or Twitter or Facebook, you could have a higher score than somebody who has a little influence but spread out on more social networks. We look at each network completely independently. The kinds of behaviors that help make you influential on Twitter make you annoying on Facebook. We do a lot of work to properly weight the value of each network for every person."

In his experiment on improving a Klout score, Neelu Modali, a consultant with SoMeGo in Washington, D.C., spent a lot of time at the beginning of the process surrounding himself with people who took a genuine interest in him. "Of the three Klout scoring factors, amplification is probably the easiest one to work with," he said. "And that depends on finding people who are likely to be interested in what you have to say.

"The more people you talk to and the more people who respond to you, the more likely you are to get amplified. And when you provide these people with meaningful content stacked on top of that, you are going to be heard and probably heard more than once as the content gets shared. The more consistent you are with your network, the more likely you are to make that amplification even stronger because you are gaining credibility."

Modali's network strategy included identifying several Twitter Chats that were routinely attended by people who shared his passion for technology, innovation, marketing, and social media. As he participated in these conversation streams, like-minded people were naturally attracted to his ideas and content. There was also a high probability that those relevant and engaged people would follow him back because he made an attempt to connect with them authentically. In other words, he was finding the least passive people in his network.

"My first mission was finding that core group of people who would be my repeaters for my message," he said. "Through the Twitter Chats, I looked for people who liked to have a discourse online. I was lucky to find some really smart people who appreciated it when I had something meaningful to say."

Other sources of relevant followers might include blog communities that interest you, LinkedIn Groups, industry forums, and topical Twitter lists.

Creating an effective presence on social networks is a fairly mature topic that has been extensively covered in the existing literature on social media marketing. Here are a few books on this topic that I recommend:

- *Six Pixels of Separation* by Mitch Joel
- *Engage* by Brian Solis
- *No Bullshit Social Media* by Jason Falls and Erik Deckers

Also, for some Twitter-specific network-building strategies, my book *The Tao of Twitter* has more than a dozen ideas to attract meaningful targeted followers.

Step 2: Have a Strategy to Provide Compelling Content

You only have a high Klout score if you're creating good content.
—JOE FERNANDEZ

The second foundational element of online influence is content. Having a strategy to develop and/or curate exceedingly useful, helpful, interesting, and entertaining content is essential to driving the specific kind of online influence measured by a Klout score.

"There are lots of ways to generate content," Neelu Modali said. "Some folks will send out a gazillion messages about articles they found online, and that's really their contribution. And there are other people who will generate original content from their blogs and still others who will shoot comments back and forth in sort of a debate. There's different types of motivations as to why you may be posting, and I think ultimately that has influence on Klout. I do think there is an emphasis on original content rather than just sending out links all day."

During this period Modali found that creating original content through a blog was a key element for success. "With new blog content, my social media connections could engage with me based on my original thinking—what I was writing about. There were lots of tweets and comments about these posts, which helps the amplification; there was definitely an impact from starting the blog. To get even more attention, I intentionally wrote some posts that were provocative and controversial. I don't intend for my blog to be that way in the long term, but I was experimenting, and it did get people to be more reactive. My initial goal for the blog was to purposefully promote Twitter activity. As I tone down the rhetoric, it may affect my Klout score, but I am also engaging with people in many other ways now, too."

Modali continued, "I used several tools to study the content of people with very high Klout scores, and they seemed to have a very even distribution of the types of content they were sharing: a combination of links, retweets, original content, replies, mentions, whatever. Quite a bit of variety. A lot of engagement, not just links."

"Another way quality content affects your score is that it lasts longer," he said. "I found that if your message survives and gets passed along for a few days, it really rocks your amplification on Klout. So you have to come up with some sort of qualitative, provocative thought to accomplish that, but the second philosophy revolves around how long your message can last on Twitter. How many times can it be reflected and bounced from person to person? And as your content is moving through that social media universe, how many of those people are going to latch on to you and deem you as somebody worthy of following?"

To really drive influence, you can't be part of the flock of sheep. After all, you're trying to influence, right? Whether you're sharing links or commenting on your day, you need to make it stand out. Don't share the link that everyone else in your network is sharing; find something new. People are much more likely to click and retweet if you're adding something of value that they haven't already seen. Likewise, if you're sharing about your day, find a way to make that hamburger or that new movie you viewed seem different and interesting.

If you're serious about increasing your Klout score, you must also be consistent. To compete, you must tweet, post, link, comment, or blog. This aspect of Klout is one of its most controversial: If you stop participating in the social web for even a few days while you go on vacation, your score begins to drop. Although your potential to be influential in real life doesn't drop if you leave for the beach for a few days, Klout justifies the practice with an analogy: If you stopped communicating at work, you wouldn't be influential there either. Since Klout can only measure your ability to create and move content, if the content is not being created, they have nothing to measure. So, simply tweeting and posting on a regular basis is part of the battle.

Klout's "official" position on this aspect is stated on its website:

Most people would agree that social media is rife with people trying to "game the system." We value consistency over sudden spikes as a means to verify a person's influence. The Klout Score isn't meant to be updated on an hourly or daily basis and we believe that this is a good thing. Just like Google doesn't change your page rank after a single blog post or you would never expect your credit score to change after paying a single bill, we do not believe a single retweet from an influencer should significantly impact your score. Every time we process your score we look back over the last 30 days to generate a holistic view of your activity and overall influence.

When it comes to ideal content, there is no magic formula. One person's network may enjoy your personal anecdotes and stories. Another might enjoy insights on sports. We've already seen how folks can become influential by sharing coupons and recipes. Follow your passion and have fun with your online engagement!

We covered many content-related ideas in Chapter 5, but here are some additional resources that will help you connect to your world with great content:

- *Content Rules: How to Create Killer Blogs, Podcasts, Videos, Ebooks, Webinars (and More) That Engage Customers and Ignite Your Business* by Anne Handley and C. C. Chapman
- *Launch* by Michael A. Stelzner
- *Content Strategy for the Web* by Christina Halvorson

Step 3: Systematically Engage Influencers Who Are Most Willing (or Least Passive) to Distribute Your Content Virally

This step is an absolutely critical one. Unless you are a true real-life celebrity (and if you are, I'd like to meet you so you can sign my book), it doesn't make any difference how big your network is or how good your content is if it is not activated by engaging with people in such a way that your content moves across the web. That is the action Klout is trying to measure as an approximation of your influence.

Klout has made it clear that how often you engage and who you are engaging with affect your influence score. If you are able to engage with other demonstrated influencers and those influencers seem to respond to you and move your content along, this is a validation of your potential power. However, as was pointed out earlier, it's a bit incestuous because Klout determines the influencers in the first place.

"One of the core principles for Klout is that they are looking for you to engage with a high-quality group of people per their measurement—the interactions don't have to be high quantity, but they do have to be high quality," said Modali. "So you need to try to interact with people who have Klout scores higher than yours. As part of my engagement strategy, I started increasing my network by connecting with people who had a higher Klout score. If my Klout was sitting at 40, I made it a point to engage with people who were sitting at 50. If my Klout was at 50, I was trying to talk to people at 70, trying to convince them that I was a smart guy and worthy of conversation. However, I hit a wall with people who had scores in the 80s. Very difficult to engage because of all the competing attention for their time."

Another idea to spur engagement is to connect online with people who are already your friends offline and to turn online connections into offline friendships. In both cases, these people will be more willing to connect and engage with you. When you are networking in real life, make sure people know how to find you across your favorite social media platforms. You might consider listing your links on the back of your business card, on your website, or in your e-mail correspondence.

Nate Riggs, a blogger and digital marketing manager for Bob Evans Restaurants, offers a few ideas on how to spark engagement with your audience:

1. *Ask earnest questions.* Asking your followers questions is a great way to start conversations. I'm always surprised at the number of people who are willing to share their thoughts on

just about anything you ask. The key is to be earnest and genuine. In other words, ask questions you really want to know the answer to. Most folks have become pretty savvy at ignoring loaded questions that are designed to promote your own objectives. For bonus points, ask questions that matter to you on a personal level. At the end of the day, we're all human, right? Humans enjoy talking to other humans about the stuff that makes us human. Don't be afraid to get personal.

2. *Try participating in a Twitter Chat.* Once you have established some consistency and expectations among your audience, organized Twitter Chats are a great way to increase the number of folks who reply to your @name or even retweet (RT) the questions and content you push out. Both of these metrics are included in what Klout looks at to determine your score. Twitter Chats are also a great way to find like-minded people to include in your online tribe. To find an updated list of Twitter Chat times and topics, simply do a search for "Twitter Chats."

3. *Show appreciation individually.* Appreciation opens more conversations on social networks. Simply saying thank you is powerful. In terms of your Klout score, each thank you message you send counts as a one-to-one conversation with one of your followers. Each one-to-one conversation you have, in turn, affects your overall score. Often, people (including me) will thank multiple followers in a single tweet. That's okay, but be aware that by doing that you are also reducing the amount of @reply's that are counted in your overall Klout score. Doing more one-to-one appreciation can give your Klout score a boost over time.

4. *Be witty and fun.* A large part of participating on Twitter lies in the entertainment value. Twitter in a sense has replaced much of the lighthearted conversations that used to take place at the water cooler. Don't feel like you have to be too reserved when you tweet. Carefully placed witty comments tend to draw a big response from followers. This also makes using Twitter much more fun, and we humans have a tendency to engage more in the places where we enjoy ourselves.

5. *Cut the noise with lists and columns.* Using tools such as HootSuite and TweetDeck gives you an advantage because you can set up specific columns for the lists you follow to make Twitter friends on those lists more visible. Taking the time to set up lists as columns in your dashboard to capture

the people you find most interesting or have the best relationships with helps you avoid missing opportunities to join their conversations. Some listening platforms allow you to sort your followers by Klout score.

6. *Brevity increases sharing.* Twitter has a 140-character limit on tweets. If you are distributing links to blog content, videos, or articles, you will automatically lose up to 10 to 15 characters. Now consider what happens when you retweet content. You lose even more through the insertion of "RT @name." To increase the shareability of your content across Twitter, try keeping your content sharing messages under 70 characters. Doing so will make it easier for multiple people to retweet your stuff. The more RTs you get, the higher your Klout score will climb.

7. *Make time for social media.* Klout does a fantastic job of measuring how humans use Twitter and other platforms to communicate with other humans. All influence is rooted in communication. But what does that really mean? It's simple. If you want to improve your influence on Twitter, it's absolutely necessary to use Twitter frequently as a day-to-day communication tool, much like e-mail, Facebook, or your mobile phone.

Other Tips and Observations to Lift your Klout Score

In May 2010, the academic paper "Measuring User Influence in Twitter: The Million Follower Fallacy"[2] made the following observations:

- Popular users who have lots of followers are not necessarily influential in terms of spawning retweets or mentions.
- The most influential users can have significant influence over a variety of topics.
- Influence is not gained spontaneously or accidentally but through concerted effort that is aided by limiting tweets to a single topic.

---

2. Meeyoung Cha, Hamed Haddadi, Fabricio Benevenuto, and Krishna P. Gummadi presented this academic paper at the Fourth Annual International AAAI Conference on Weblogs and Social Media (ICWSM) in May 2010.

It makes sense. Unless you are a social media superstar with thousands of engaged and diverse followers hanging on your every word, the audience you built because of your expertise in Formula One racing or knitting is probably going to yawn over your opinions on the latest trends in fine dining. Make sure to limit your topics.

There is also an emerging science around optimizing tweets for maximum potential exposure and sharing. Free software applications like Buffer can help determine when most of your followers are online and help you plan your tweeting most efficiently.

The +K

In 2011, Klout introduced the +K: a way to acknowledge that somebody is influential to you in a certain subject or topic. Clicking on the +K button next to a person's profile on the Klout site quickly became a popular gesture to acknowledge his or her expertise and helpfulness. But many wondered, What impact does someone clicking your +K button have on your actual Klout score?

"The +K doesn't affect your score," said Fernandez. "We put it out for a few reasons. First, to drive engagement with our site, and second, to help build our models around influence topics. For example, my friend influences me about things like cars or wine, so giving him +K acknowledges that. If I came to your hometown and you recommended a restaurant to me and I went there and enjoyed it, I should be able to give you a +K to acknowledge that gesture. If I'm sitting at a conference and listening to a panel where somebody is making amazing points I never thought of, I should be able to give them a +K and reward them.

"We would like to add it as a factor eventually, but the integrity of the score is so important, so we have to take baby steps. We're analyzing the data. We have to just be smart as to how we include +K, if it ever gets included at all."

And the Results Are In . . .

In his quest for Klout, Neelu Modali spent between one and three hours a day on the project for 45 days, working his network, creating content, and connecting with influencers. The result? He raised his score from 39 to 69.

"The largest gains came early on," he said, "and I admit I had some cynicism around the whole thing because it seemed that Klout scores could be so easily moved! But as my data footprint online grew larger, it became more and more difficult for me to move my Klout score forward. When you have a larger data pool, the system becomes more accurate as it draws conclusions from more of your content and interactions."

Moldani was obsessed with beating the system, but was there more to it than that? Is it possible that while attempting to become more active and interactive, he actually became more influential?

"That's an interesting question," he said. "I did set out to game the system. But during the process, I also developed amazing relationships with some great new friends. And they do seem to care about what I have to say, and they act on it. My conclusion for my little Klout science fair project is that actually I am more influential today because I set out to increase my Klout score.

"My hypothesis was that there are three or four factors I can manipulate to move my score up quickly. I was right about that, but the real conclusion is that through this process, I have met and engaged with people who are high value to me personally. They have relevance to my world and are relationships I will carry forward. So yes, the irony is that as I raised my score, I became more influential."

No Klout-enhancement strategy is going to be perfect because of the ever-changing complexity of the system. "We are constantly adding measurement factors," said Klout CEO Joe Fernandez. "Our science team of 10 people—that's their job every day—refines that algorithm and makes it better. We've come to the conclusion that all of these social networks are different, so we have built every algorithm associated with them case by case. There are different factors of influence for every channel. For example, some normal interaction might come across as annoying on Facebook.

"And then we have another algorithm that combines the scores for you—not generically for everybody but specifically for you and the way you show up on the social web. So if your most effective platform is Facebook, that will take up the bulk of your scoring and everything else is added in. Eventually the algorithm will be hundreds of data points, even thousands at some point. It's infinite complexity.

"Look at the journey Google began in 1997. Constant improvement for search . . . constant ideas to make it even better. That's the journey we will be on too. Forever."

CHAPTER 11

The Future of Social Scoring

paigecraig paigecraig
Looking at @BetterWorks job applications - just saw a
resume with the persons @Klout score emphasized - Nice
idea!
23 Feb

Our *Return on Influence* journey has taken us through the
history of influence marketing, swirled all around classical notions of influence, scaled the heights of content,
and clambered all over Klout. There's only one place left
to go: the future!

Let's drive this bus over to a few new stops and take a look at
where social scoring may be heading. Here are views from the people who would know best.

Credit for Your Content

Azeem Azhar, Founder of PeerIndex

"There's a single driving force behind this social scoring trend, and
that is to help people reclaim their data and the value of that data,"
said Azeem Azhar.

"All of us have been giving away our data and our content for a
very long time. Now companies need to find ways to help people
create value for that data. And when I talk about value, it's not in a
Twitter kind of way where a service will help you get more followers, so you can get more followers, so you can get more followers!

I mean value in a deep and meaningful way where you get a letter from American Airlines saying, 'You don't fly with us very often, but you are exactly the type of customer we would love to have in the fold. Please accept this free flight as a way for you to get to know us and an opportunity to earn your business.'

"Right now the trade-off is so against the individual consumer that it is unfair. Data and content are being used behind our backs for sort of banal, not very meaningful targeting. Let's stop that."

"To get there," Azhar explained, "one asset we're trying to build at PeerIndex is a competency to understand and profile customers across many facets of a person's behavior and interactions. We know companies are very keen to understand their customers. For example, we are working with a record label to help them understand the profiles of who is actually following them on Twitter or Facebook. If you have a million followers, what does that mean? Who are the true influencers, and what is that worth? Is that worth $50 to a brand or $50,000? Unless you can figure out how to define that by certain parameters and sort it, you would never have any idea.

"Think about the potential application to your inbound sales leads. What if you could assess their online behavior in such a way that you could begin to predict who is most likely to buy? So now we have 100 sales leads to evaluate. If we have limited resources, which ones should we respond to immediately—with a discount to earn their business—and which ones should we respond to in sort of a normal period of time? If you could refine that assessment and prove—through actual sales conversions—that you're correct, you would have a strong case for what the ROI will be of such a system.

"Eventually it is our ambition to be able to assign a specific potential value to each sales lead, person by person, and reward the leads appropriately. Maybe you could determine that Person A is believed to be worth $120 in potential sales, so a sales agent would be authorized to spend $19 to go after him and still make a profit."

"Ultimately," he continued, "if you could use these data to also judge that person's ability to influence, you could assess not only their specific dollar value but a probable dollar value in referral sales.

"Here's an example of how this influence data could be used in a very real way. I saw a very interesting piece of research about how people buy iPhones. A person who didn't know anybody who owned an iPhone was only half as likely to buy one in the next six months compared to somebody who knew two people who owned one. By the time you knew five people with an iPhone, you were just going to buy one.

"It turns out that when we start to evaluate influence within the pattern of market consumption, it's not really just about your influence score but more about the subject of influence and the impact it has on the people around you. The technology is progressing to the point that we are beginning to have the ability to measure that.

"Part of the journey is to be in a place where we can answer the most meaningful question, which is, 'So what?' How am I going to get Bob to actually buy an iPhone? If I identified two people who can persuade Bob, now that would make it really interesting. And what if we could determine how many messages Bob would need to see or what kind of trusted person needs to be in contact with Bob before he decides this is something he needs to do?"

"You're not going to get that by looking at a single user's score," he said. "You would have to understand the network structure, the influence of the complex interactions in the network. And that is taking the field to another level. That's where we need to be."

Beyond Just Buzz

Tom Webster, Vice President, Edison Research

"Measures like Klout are going to take off when they can show the link to other key business metrics," said Tom Webster. "It's an iterative thing. Klout is getting better and may get to a level someday of the Net Promoter Score (a customer loyalty metric based on how likely you are to recommend a product to a friend). But like Net Promoter, the real magic is going to come when you can correlate metrics from Klout with other key measurements of your brand.

"For instance, Net Promoter Scores within the airline industry correlate with other measurements like customer satisfaction surveys, which in turn correlate well with frequent flyer or loyalty programs and repeat business. They have done the work and have demonstrated the linkage. Once companies start doing that for Klout—and I think they will—people will begin to believe in the system and rely on Klout for having internal consistency. Then the returns really start to be significant when you can show the linkage between somebody who has a high Klout score and some corresponding loyalty or buying behavior."

"An important point is that this will become granular by topic," Webster said, "and vary topic by topic. And some topics will lend themselves to correlation better than others."

The Promise of Local

Neelu Modali, Consultant with SoMeGo

"Countries like India have skipped right over the broadband revolution and have gone right to the 3G revolution," Modali explained. "Everybody is constantly connected to the world by their cell phone, so there is this continuous tracking of where people are, what they are doing, what movie they're watching, what car they're buying. People are even riding around on their motorcycles and talking on their cell phones.

"If you want to see where this influence trend is going, look to emerging markets like India and the importance of geolocation.

"In the city of Hyderabad, where most of my family lives, the traffic is abysmal. It takes you an hour to go even a few miles. Everybody is at a standstill in one location, talking or texting on their phones or some device. Local shop owners really have an opportunity. If I'm a coffee shop owner, I should really offer these people sitting in their car across the street a deal, especially if I know they love coffee. We're getting to a point where we will be able to leverage some predictive abilities to determine where people are going to be and who among them are coffee aficionados, high-value users, influencers, or even my competitor's customer."

"Even though you may not have this extreme example of Hyderabad, where it's like an online stream literally taking place in front of you," Modali continued, "there are still potential customers around your store all the time, and they are getting to the point of constant connectivity, too. What if you could assess the nearby social stream by different variables—find the people who are looking for something to eat, somebody having a problem with their car—and connect to them on the spot?

"As far as innovations go, I would look for mathematical models to better evaluate the quality of content, the origination of content, and how far and fast an echo can spread. I would also look at combining topics and location: Are people consistently talking about the same topics from the same places or from different places? A lot can be done to integrate with Foursquare."

Computer Code Plus Genetic Code

Paul Saarinen, Director of Digital Insights and Culture for Bolin Marketing

Saarinen had this to say about the future of social scoring: "What I really love to see is a data mash-up between Klout and 23andMe, a company that does genetic testing for health, disease, and ancestry. What if we could connect influence, interests, and behavior patterns to the genetic code? What if you could connect the dots between genotype reports and behavior? I think you would see some interesting correlations there."

Connecting Online Conversations with Offline Behavior

Robert Scoble, Technology Blogger

Robert Scoble said, "I think the technology is getting to a point where you will be able to connect online conversations with offline behaviors. It's already getting pretty close to that for me. I have 1,700 check-ins on Foursquare, so people can see my history and a map of where I've been in the world. People can certainly see your patterns of behavior with applications like Foodspotting or other programs that can even capture things like how many calories you're eating in a day. Other applications can track how I exercise, what music I listen to, and where I ride on my bike. So more and more offline activities are being recorded online, at least if you're the kind of person who wants to track those things."

"That information alone does not represent influence since that's all about getting other people to take action," Scoble explained. "But what if you are talking about a movie online and then lots of people who follow you check in at that movie? Or they buy your favorite music? What if you recommend a restaurant and people who are strongly connected to you tweet from that restaurant? We are certainly going to be able to connect those dots.

"Brands want to know who is moving the needle—at least the big brands are at this point. A company recently told me exactly how many people are visiting their website based on something I wrote. So they are following this carefully. That is very, very valuable information, and that's how they decide who gets access.

"One technology company I visited had monitors on their walls that tracked all of the social media activity for their brand names. They could follow traffic spikes and then determine what happened.

Did a tech publication write about us? Did Oprah talk about us? The best companies are all tracking that and building good PR strategies around that. And then the good PR companies are tracking those influencers and grouping people who are most likely to move the needle."

Klout Everywhere

Joe Fernandez, CEO of Klout

"We want to think of influence the way Google thought of maps," said Fernandez. "Google made it easy to use their maps in many ways, and now developers have taken mapping and used it in creative applications you never would have thought about. We are looking at making influence available to the world. We talk about unlocking the world's influence.

"How it will be used? I didn't think about hotels using it to upgrade rooms when I started it, but it's certainly becoming a common thing. We talk about using your phone to generate location-based influence offers.

"How do we help the restaurant that just opened find the 10 coolest people in the neighborhood they need to get to try their food so they can get good word of mouth going? We can definitely enable that. Another idea I like: When I slide my credit card at any register, my Klout score should come up and they should be able to see, 'Wow, we have a whale here, and so I'm going to go above and beyond to make sure this person has a good experience.' Maybe carry their bag to the car or give them a bounce-back coupon or even just remember their name and get to know them. I think Klout can enable that in the not too distant future.

"Internally, we talk about Klout becoming part of the fabric of the social web. I want everybody to be touching it. So when I land on the *LA Times* news page and they know my Klout score is big when it comes to technology, why don't they show the technology page first? And if they know that I share everything on Twitter, why not do away with the other buttons and just have a big Twitter button? Why not show a car ad that I can interact with and get a major benefit because of my Klout score?

"Every website should be able to be customized based on what I'm influential about and who I influence. Klout becomes your personal VIP pass to the world. Could you even use Klout as currency? It has infinite possibilities."

The Digital Layer and Beyond

Mark Schaefer, Author of This Book

Of course I want to join in the fun of thinking through where these trends could lead. There are some interesting intersections ahead.

Convergence with Augmented Reality

What happens when Klout scores are all around you? When people can judge you by holding up a smartphone and having a number hover over your head? It's going to happen, probably within the next few years.

Augmented reality provides a digital layer over the real world that you view through a mobile device and eventually through eyeglasses. For example, if you're fixing a car, you could see a digital layer over your actual car showing you what step to take next. An illustration of a rocket ship could ignite and take off from a children's book. Digital docents can show you around an art museum or monstrous characters can interact with you in your own neighborhood, as projected through these applications.

What happens when you can go a bar, or a job interview, or the high school dance and somebody is seeing your latest social stream—and Klout score—hovering around you?

New Business Generation

In 2009, when Twitter was first gathering steam, I saw a chart depicting nearly 300 third-party applications to help you manage your tweets, followers, and any other aspect of personal Twitter enhancement you could imagine. It was pretty impressive that this struggling little application was already spawning so much innovation!

How many new businesses can be created and sustained with access to influence scores? Why wouldn't there be an online application to coach you through a process of increasing your score? When will the first personal Klout coaches hit the market?

New competitors to Klout and PeerIndex are emerging every week. How will the market segment and fracture? Will there be social scoring platforms specifically for teenagers? For the singles dating scene? In late 2011, a Silicon Valley start-up called CrushBlvd might have represented the first entry in this market for niche social scoring when it created a "social networking site for beautiful people." CEO Tina Lee said the aim of the new venture was to "help people find and socialize with beautiful people in a beautiful community."

Social scoring technologies are a perfect match for political campaigns. An entire industry will emerge that matches passionate influencers with political candidates. Imagine if a campaign gave free tickets to exclusive fund-raising events by using Klout scores. A new company, Votizen, launched a tool that evaluates social media followers of political candidates, cross-references the list with voting records, and suggests the high-potential voters to contact for each politician.

Calculating a Return on Influence

As companies begin to connect the dots between online influence and offline activities, real dollar values can be placed on customers and the demonstrated impact of their influence. Think of the implications for customer relationship management (CRM), sales, and customer service.

Companies have always provided different levels of service, depending on how much money a customer spends, how recently he or she has bought something, or some measure of loyalty. It makes sense to take an individual's level of influence into account. There may be debate about whether it's fair, but what is the value associated with angering a customer with a Klout score of 15 versus one with a score of 75?

In 2011 Facebook announced initiatives to make it easier to record increasing amounts of obscure personal data on the social web: the complete catalog of songs you listen to, in order; the television shows you watch each day; the events you attend. They call it the Timeline for your life, but it amounts to a record of your behavior patterns, attitudes, and buying preferences. Can there be any question that we are heading for a future in which for many of us the influence of others will absolutely be connected to our offline behaviors and beyond—even measurable changes in our attitudes and opinions?

Internal Applications to the Corporation

When the Google model began to mature, the technology was eagerly applied to corporate search needs. Google now powers the search function on many company websites as well as internal company portals.

Likewise, the popular adoption of social networking has spawned internal applications at some companies. Platforms like Yammer connect far-flung employees with familiar social communication technology.

It's not too much of a stretch to think that as offline and online behaviors begin to blur, companies could adopt something like Klout for internal performance evaluations. Could social scoring algorithms help:

- Demonstrate influence *within* a company?
- Show the ability to influence targeted customers, community power brokers, donors, and decision makers?
- Grade one aspect of leadership, communication ability, and influence with customers?

Before I was hired for a key sales position at a Fortune 100 company, I was put through a half-day of testing that generated a psychographic profile that could be compared to the most successful salespersons in the company. These scores were used to determine if I should be hired or not (I was!). Wouldn't an ability to generate online influence be a key indicator for many professional roles like customer service, sales, and public relations? Of course this would be a controversial application, but I think the trend could head in this direction.

Capitalizing on Exclusivity

Today Klout is basically a spectator sport. There is little that you can do other than watch your score rise and fall.

But when are clublike exclusive social networks going to form that are based on topics and Klout scores? Wouldn't access to one of these exclusive networks be a valuable perk or an effective way to connect on a continuous basis with a powerful group of engaged influencers? Would you even pay to be in an elite discussion group or business networking organization that limits membership to those with extreme influence in a specialized topic? Sort of a MENSA for baseball, investing, entrepreneurship, or whatever your passion might be? Exclusivity and scarcity are powerful motivators, as we have seen.

Social scoring is in its infancy, the silent movie stage. Who can imagine what new businesses and applications will emerge when not only do you have a return on influence but everybody else in the world does too?

CHAPTER 12

Social Influence: A Personal View

markwschaefer Mark Schaefer
The elegance of the social web is that it's shedding its skin every day.
2 minutes ago

W elcome to the end of the book. If you made it this far, you're extraordinary. I saw a statistic from Kindle showing that most business books are abandoned about one-third of the way through, so if you're on this page, congratulations and thank you. Courage now—you have just 544 words to go!

At the top of my blog *{grow}*, there are three words: Marketing, Social Media, Humanity. These words ignite passion in me and have fueled the love and energy that created this book, along with the fear of its consequences.

The incredible progress that has occurred in social scoring technology creates an entirely new way to connect with and reward engaged customers. It's an exhilarating prospect for those in my profession of *marketing*.

I am humbled and inspired by the opportunities presented by the new era of the Citizen Influencer that has opened the world to anybody, anywhere with the passion, presence, and persistence to be heard. We are indebted to the free, simple publishing platforms of *social media*.

This brings us to *humanity*. And this is where I am becoming queasy.

By definition, influence is elitist. If everybody were influential, nobody would be influential! So by assigning numbers to people and stacking them up in order, the system institutionalizes a culture of haves and have-nots.

Where corruption can occur, corruption will occur; of this we can be certain. Perhaps we are on the brink of a marketing arms race characterized by the uniqueness, exclusivity, and value of stuff that is being given away. If the culture of gathering this valuable merchandise builds up steam, it will undoubtedly drive some disturbing human behaviors.

The haves will rake in the goodies, and the have-nots will be resentful or embark on a campaign to buy or scheme their way to the top of the charts. Will that activity dilute the effectiveness of these new marketing channels? Will it drive unethical black hat games among those who are eager to serve the wealthy and desperate?

Common, free applications already enable us to sort social media content streams and customer complaint queues by levels of influence as determined by Klout. In effect, this sorting keeps people in their place. The bourgeois can keep the proletariat out of contention. The very technologies lifting up these amazing Citizen Influencers can be used to repress newcomers so that their messages are seldom heard. The mechanics of oppression have always been fairly simple. The elite form a pack that systematically manipulates the resources among a chosen few in a way that keeps the rabble out.

And when that happens, there's a revolution.

The elegance of the social web is that it is shedding its skin every day. It's a constantly evolving organism, squirming and writhing its way toward its next innovation. The Internet is the most customer-sensitive business platform in history. If a product or service loses sight of the incredible power of these new influencers, a challenger will eventually be assembled and embraced.

Yes, we are numbers now. Unavoidably, we will be known for our Klout scores and followers and badges of social proof. But the smartest marketers will always remember that we are people too.

The ongoing tension between the opportunity of influence and the demand for humanity is far too significant to remain unresolved. How will it work itself out? I have no idea. But it will, and the story will probably make a great book. I think I'll call it *The New Return on Influence: You* Were *a Number*.

Thank you for reading my book. Stay in touch, won't you?

The Social Media Primer

I f you're unfamiliar with social media or are just starting out, it will be helpful to become familiar with a few basic terms and concepts. Don't worry. I'll bring you up to speed in no time and help you understand the terminology and ideas in the book.

Social media has radically changed the way people and businesses communicate. Before social media came along, businesses relied on one-way communication and "push" marketing tactics to get the word out about their brands. Traditional media channels such as television, radio, print publications, billboards, and direct mail dominated the marketer's playbook. Businesses focused heavily on messaging and brand recognition to drive sales.

Then social media came along, creating a seismic shift in the way we communicate. Instead of the one-to-many mass marketing of traditional media, businesses can now communicate with consumers on a person-to-person level. Unlike traditional media channels, social media have placed an incredible amount of power in the hands of the consumer. Now, for the first time, consumers have the ability to talk back to brands through Twitter, Facebook, and review sites instead of only being on the receiving end of the marketing message.

To take that a step further, consumers can also start the conversation about a brand. Whether a business is involved in social media or not, consumers still have the ability to talk about it—publicly—online. With the advent of widely available Internet access and free social media platforms, everyone can be a publisher now.

This phenomenon has amplified the importance of word-of-mouth marketing. Of course word of mouth has existed as long as marketplaces and products have existed. But now, instead of telling one or two friends about your new cell phone, you can tell hundreds or thousands of your social media contacts in a matter of seconds. In fact, many consumers may have bigger online audiences than do the brands themselves. Pretty eye-opening, isn't it?

Brands that understand how to harness the power of social media are rewarded with legions of fans and followers who are quick to defend these companies or organizations when people come with torches and pitchforks. However, social media also has the ability to bring a business to its knees by publicly showcasing its flaws and missteps.

So, what is social media? And how does it all work? Buckle your seat belt and we'll quickly get you up to speed about the social media landscape today.

What Is Social Media?

Before I explain the different social media channels, it's important to understand what makes social media different from traditional media. Social media is all the following:

Interactive. Perhaps the hallmark of social media is that it gives people and businesses the ability to participate in public two-way conversations. Before social media, businesses relied on focus groups, surveys, and sales numbers to get feedback from their customers. Now all they have to do is take a look online to put their finger on the pulse of customer ideas, feedback, and conversations.

In fact, many businesses are using social media as a means to respond to customer complaints and even troubleshoot problems from afar. Ford, AT&T, Comcast, and Bank of America are examples of powerhouse brands that have Twitter accounts dedicated to customer service. Most large companies use powerful social media listening platforms to gauge consumer sentiment, look for trouble spots, and respond to questions and comments.

Free (mostly). A common thread among social networks is that they all have the same price point—zero. You may not have to pay to create a social profile, but that does not mean social media is entirely free. It's important to remember that although the social networks may be free, your time is not, and some of this work can be labor-intensive. A brand such as McDonald's, for example, has a team of people resourcing Twitter most hours of the day and in several languages. Tracking and monitoring tools and other applications that can enhance your social media experience often come with a cost as well.

Real time. Thanks to social media, you can get the message out about your brand instantly. There's no other communication channel that works nearly as fast as social media. Social media operates in real time, and so you can literally see what people are saying, doing, and thinking across the globe right now.

Here's a famous, creative example of how a brand integrated traditional planned advertising with a social media component. Procter & Gamble devised a humorous over-the-top television advertising campaign for the Old Spice brand featuring actor Isaiah Mustafa as "the Man Your Man Could Smell Like." The popular character came to life as people could interact with him on Twitter and Facebook. He even answered questions posed to him through Twitter over a series of rapid-fire YouTube videos. This integration significantly enhanced the product's brand awareness and engaged customers for a fraction of the cost of the original commercials.

Everyone publishes. The power of social media is that it gives everyone a microphone. You don't have to be a member of the press or have a multimillion-dollar advertising budget to reach consumers. You only need a computer or cell phone. Social media gives everyone a voice, including your competitors, customers, and employees.

Mobile. As the number of smartphone users continues to grow, so does social media use on cell phones. People have the ability to share messages, photos, and videos from their smartphones. No computer required.

Public. Although this depends largely on the social network and a user's privacy settings, much of social media happens in broad daylight for the world to see. And much of this information is findable in search engines.

Social Media Platforms

To understand social media and the arguments and conclusions in this book, it is helpful to have a basic grasp of the various social media platforms and the unique language associated with each of them. Let's take a spin through some of the most popular platforms mentioned in the book.

Blogs

The oldest form of social media, blogs give the average web user the ability to publish long-form content quickly and easily. As opposed to static websites, blogs are interactive in nature, allowing visitors to leave a comment on individual articles or blog posts. Many newspaper websites now operate like blogs as readers have the ability to post comments on articles.

Blogs began as online diaries, giving people the ability to share their thoughts and ideas online. However, in time, blogs grew in popularity and became a common and powerful tool used by businesses. In fact, many company websites are built on blogging platforms to allow website owners to upload content easily.

Twitter

Twitter is the darling of bloggers, celebrities, and members of the media thanks to its in-the-moment and public nature. Unless you choose to keep your messages private, everything you post on Twitter is available for the world to see. In today's social media–driven world, breaking news often comes in the form of a tweet. Twitter is also searchable, which makes it easy for users to find information about various topics and for businesses to monitor what people are saying about their brands.

To get a handle on how Twitter works, here is a quick rundown of its key functionality:

Tweets. A post on Twitter is called a tweet. Tweets must be 140 characters or less; this allows them to be distributed via text message on a cell phone.

Timeline. Your timeline, or stream, shows all the tweets for the people you are following on Twitter. Tweets will show up in your stream in real time, and so you can literally see what the world is talking about right now.

Follow/unfollow. Although anyone can see your tweets by looking at your profile page, you must "follow" a Twitter user to see his or her updates in your timeline. The people who follow someone on Twitter are called followers. If you no longer want to see someone's tweets in your stream, you can unfollow that person at any time. Unlike on Facebook, you can see a timeline of anybody you follow without that person following you back.

@replies. Part of the beauty of Twitter is the ability to engage in two-way conversations. You can do this by sending an @reply. For instance, if you see that your friend Bob tweeted about his barbecue on Saturday, you can send him an @reply to let him know you'll be coming. Bob will be notified of the tweet, and he'll see it in his @ mentions tab on Twitter. These tweets are public and form the large database that is mined by companies such as Klout as they dissect and categorize your content.

Direct message. If you want to communicate with someone privately on Twitter, you can send that person a direct message (DM). This works much like an e-mail or a text except that the person you send the message to can read the message. One important thing to note is that you can send a direct message only to a person who is following you on Twitter.

Retweets. A retweet (RT) is a way to forward or share a message that you found on Twitter. Think of it as being like forwarding an e-mail you received to your contacts. In Twitter vernacular, a retweet is denoted with "RT" at the beginning of a tweet. In the world of social scoring, retweets are important because they show that somebody else is sharing your content; you have influenced that person to do something.

URL shorteners. Because Twitter limits tweets to 140 characters, URL shorteners can be used to shrink a website address so that it can be easily shared in a tweet. Third-party programs allow you track how many times people click or share a link.

Avatar. An avatar is the photo or image uploaded to your Twitter account. Your avatar shows up next to your tweets in the Twitter stream.

Lists. Twitter allows you to group users into lists, and that helps you sort and organize your Twitter experience. You can add people to a list even if you don't follow them. Your profile shows the number of times you've been added to a list. You can click on that number to see the different lists you've been added to. Additionally, people can look at the lists you've created unless you choose to keep them private.

Facebook

What began as a network for college students has transformed into the biggest social network and the largest website in the world. In my classes, I teach that Facebook isn't a website but a lifestyle. These days, everyone and her mother, grandmother, uncle, and cousin twice removed is on Facebook, as it has become a popular mechanism for helping people stay connected by sharing photos, videos, and information with one another.

Here is a quick look at Facebook's key functionality:

Status update. Whereas Twitter has tweets, Facebook has status updates. Facebook users can post a simple text message or include a link, photo, or video with their status updates. Facebook limits status updates to 420 characters, which is significantly larger than the character limit on Twitter.

Wall. Every Facebook profile comes with a wall that includes status updates, photos, videos, and the user's activity throughout Facebook. The wall also allows visitors, depending on the privacy settings, to post messages there.

Friends. Facebook operates on the idea of mutual consent through "friending." If you want to see updates on Facebook from another user, you must friend each other. In other words, one user must send a friend request to another user, and the second user has the option to accept or deny that request.

News Feed. Much like Twitter's timeline, the Facebook News Feed offers all the status updates, photos, and videos your friends posted to Facebook.

Likes. The "like" button allows you to endorse or like everything from a status update to a photo or company page. Facebook's infamous "like" button extends beyond the walls of Facebook and onto all sorts of sites across the web. However, when you like a page outside of Facebook, that activity will still show up on your Facebook wall.

Pages. Companies that live in Facebook do so through pages. Company pages do not require that you approve a friend request. A user simply has to click the "like" button on a company page to receive information from that business in the user's Facebook News Feed.

LinkedIn

LinkedIn is considered the social network for professionals. LinkedIn showcases your businesses experience and connects you with contacts from your e-mail address book and places you've worked.

LinkedIn Profiles are much like an online résumé, detailing your education, skills, and experience, along with recommendations from your colleagues and friends. It also gives you the opportunity to link to presentations, blog posts, and your portfolio. Like the other social networks, LinkedIn allows you to post a status update on the site, which can include a link.

Your friends on LinkedIn are called connections. Much like Facebook, LinkedIn requires that people have mutual consent to connect with one another. In other words, if you want to connect with someone on LinkedIn, he or she must approve your request to connect. Once you are connected with someone on LinkedIn, you have the ability to see the person's full profile and see his or her updates in the network activity area of your dashboard.

Foursquare

Although there are a number of location-based social networks, such as Gowalla, Brightkite, and Loopt, Foursquare remains king.

Location-based social networks emphasize sharing information on the basis of your current location. Foursquare in particular works as a game that awards points and badges for users "checking in" to various locations. The person who checks into a place the most is deemed the mayor of that place.

Although Foursquare may sound like a silly game, it has become a great way to market local businesses and encourage brand loyalty. In fact, many businesses offer specials to the mayor of their establishment or users who have checked in a certain number of times.

You also have the ability to attach a location to your Facebook updates and Twitter tweets. The ability to determine your location through these online platforms could form an important link between online content and offline activities that would determine true influence.

Google+

Google+ may be one of the newer kids on the social media block, but it is the fastest growing, as it amassed 10 million users in its first 16 days. That's something that took Twitter and Facebook more than two years to do.

There are a few things that distinguish it from the other social networks. First, Google+ allows you to share a status update, photo, or video with certain contacts or groups, called circles. Also, the Google+ Stream offers threaded conversations, much like Facebook's News Feed. However, Google+ does not limit the length of status updates as Twitter and Facebook do.

Google+ also stands apart because it extends beyond status updates and profiles. The service has incorporated group video chats called Hangouts, group texting called Huddle, and a content feed based on interest called Sparks.

Google+ has also created the "+1" button, which allows the user to +1 a status update or comment or even content on websites outside of Google+. This works much like the Facebook "like" button; the key difference is that the "+1" button may have an impact on a user's search results, though Google has been tight-lipped about the implications of the button.

Flickr

Photo sharing is one of the most popular activities on the web. Although photo sharing is incorporated into most social networks, Flickr is entirely dedicated to sharing and displaying photos.

Flickr offers a nice slide show capability, which is a great feature for professional photographers and those who want an inexpensive way to include a photo slide show on their own websites. Flickr is interactive, giving users the ability to comment and download photos. The site also provides a robust search engine that allows users to find photos by keyword.

YouTube

People love viewing and sharing videos online. In fact, more than 2 billion videos are viewed on YouTube every day.

YouTube and sites such as Vimeo, Dailymotion, and Veoh give people the ability to upload, search, view, and share online videos. The content can range from newscasts and business videos to personal and family videos.

There you have it. If you're new to the world of social media and this seems confusing, don't worry. The book doesn't get into too much technical complexity, and I think you'll be able to follow along.

Platforms That Measure Influence

There are a number of websites and platforms that attempt to measure online personal influence, and the list is growing every day. To help you get a grasp on the various tools available, I've pulled together a list of the most popular sites that measure influence, with a brief overview of each one:

BackTweets. BackTweets is primarily an analytics tool, but it also includes a proprietary scoring algorithm in its dashboard that awards influence scores between 1 and 100. It shows the sites a user shares the most, along with the people the user influences and who the user is influenced by. There is limited functionality to the free version, but there is also a subscription option:

http://backtweets.com

Booshaka. This platform focuses entirely on providing intelligence and metrics around Facebook. It offers a free Facebook plug-in called Top Fans that creates a leaderboard of your most active Facebook fans. Fans also receive Booshaka points on the basis of the quality of their participation. The pro version of the product gives a business the ability to offer rewards to its top fans. The basic app is free, and pro versions cost up to $2,000 per month:

http://www.booshaka.com/

Empire Avenue. Primarily a measure of popularity and persistence, Empire Avenue is a free online game. Instead of letting you buying shares in the stock market, Empire Avenue gives you the ability to invest fake money (Eaves) in people online. Your initial share price is based on your activity in each of your social networks. From there, your online behavior on Empire Avenue, investment activity, and other social networks will dictate the rise and fall of your portfolio value:

http://empireavenue.com/

Klout. Considered the most prominent site that measures influence by virtue of its widespread use, Klout assigns a score from 1 to 100 that is based on dozens of variables that measure true reach, amplification probability, and network score across numerous social platforms.

In its scoring dashboard, Klout offers a list of topics a user is influential about and provides a list of people that user influences. Klout also assigns each user a Klout Style, which is an assessment of the user's influence style or personality.

A key differentiator with Klout is that in mid-2011, it started offering Klout Perks, which are discounts, giveaways, and special offers that are given by brands to influencers on Klout. It's free to use for participants, and the company makes money by administering the Perks Program:

http://klout.com

Kred. Much like Klout, Kred assigns each Twitter user a score from 1 to 1,000 on the basis of a user's ability to inspire action through replies, retweets, and new followers. The key differentiator between Kred and other tools is that it shows you exactly how you got your score, allowing you to see the "performance" of every tweet. It's free to use:

http://kred.ly/

My Web Career. This site analyzes Twitter, Facebook, LinkedIn, Quora, and web search results to determine a person's "career score." Your career score resembles a financial credit score, with the highest score being 850. The site also offers guidance for improving your score. Career scores and recommendations are free, but additional metrics are available if you upgrade to a paid monthly plan:

http://www.mywebcareer.com/

PeerIndex. London-based PeerIndex assigns a score, called a PeerIndex number, based on its own algorithm to measure influence. PeerIndex analyzes data from Twitter, Facebook, LinkedIn, Quora, and any URLs that you choose and assigns a score on a scale from 1 to 100.

The overall PeerIndex score is composed of scores from three areas: activity, audience, and authority. PeerIndex automatically shows your score compared with those of the people you've most recently conversed with online, and it gives you the ability to compare your score with that of others. It's free and has also introduced a perks program:

http://www.peerindex.com/

PROskore. PROskore is sort of a mash-up between Klout and LinkedIn. With the ambitious goal of wanting to "rank every professional in the world," members of the free PROskore service are rated according to reputation—which includes their social networks (LinkedIn, Facebook, Twitter)—as well as their experience and recommendations received through the PROskore community. The company aspires to help professionals prequalify sales leads and potential business partners.

www.proskore.com

ShopIgniter. Instead of simply measuring a person's overall online influence, ShopIgniter's social commerce analytics tool identifies which customers do the best job of using social media to spread the word about your business. For instance, this tool allows businesses to see which customers shared information online, who they shared it with, and the outcome of sharing that information. Additionally, this tool gives businesses the ability to reward VIPs and their most loyal customers with special discounts or access to limited-edition merchandise:

http://www.shopigniter.com/

Social Business Index. Whereas other influence tools measure personal influence, Social Business Index focuses on analyzing how effectively businesses use social media. Each business is given an index number that ranks that company's social media performance. The free site allows users to filter rankings by industry and company size and track a company's index score:

http://socialbusinessindex.com/

Social Mention. Although Social Mention is primarily used for searches and tracking, it offers a breakdown of posts by sentiment, passion, reach, and strength. Social Mention's reach score is its way of measuring influence, as it shows "the number of unique authors

referencing your brand divided by the total number of mentions." It
is a free application:
http://www.socialmention.com/

SocMetrics. SocMetrics considers itself the "topical influence platform" because it looks for social media influencers by topic. The free
site gives users the ability to search for influencers by topic and then
filter the list by keyword or location. SocMetrics also allows users
to compare their influence and social reach against those of others:
http://socmetrics.com/

Soovox. Soovox calls itself the new "influencer network." It measures
users' social IQ and then provides rewards for supporting the brands
and products they love most. The social IQ measures the ability of
a user to influence others' thoughts and actions by examining the
user's Twitter, Facebook, and LinkedIn activity:
http://soovox.com/

Sprout Social. In addition to being a social media management and
measurement tool, Sprout Social has influence and engagement
scores baked into its dashboard. Both scores are based on a scale
from 1 to 100. The dashboard also offers a Social Scorecard that
tracks new followers, mentions, message volume, and engagement.
There is a trial offer, but a paid subscription is required:
http://sproutsocial.com/

Square Grader. HubSpot's free Square Grader tool ranks your
Foursquare use on a scale from 1 to 100 and ranks you among all the
other Foursquare users that have been graded:
http://squaregrader.com/

Tweet Grader. Similar to Square Grader, Tweet Grader is a free
HubSpot tool that focuses on determining the power, reach, and
authority of your Twitter profile. It rates your Twitter profile by
assigning a grade from 1 to 100 and ranks your profile among all
other Twitter profiles that have been ranked on the site. After com-
puting your score, the site offers tips and suggestions for improving
your Twitter presence and provides a tweet cloud that shows the
topics you talk about most:
http://tweet.grader.com/

TwentyFeet. Twenty Feet uses graphs to slice and dice data from your various social networks. It measures "reputation indicators," which count the followers won and lost and the number of times a user is listed. Influence indicators measure mentions and retweets. Both free and paid accounts are available:

    https://www.twentyfeet.com/

Twitalyzer. This application offers a basic overview of a Twitter user's influence. It includes an impact score, which looks at number of followers, unique mentions, retweets, and frequency of posts. It also provides an impact percentile, which tells you where a user's impact score ranks among other Twitter users. Twitalyzer also assigns one of five influencer types: Everyday Users, Reporters, Social Butterflies, Trendsetters, and Thought Leaders. The free Twitalyzer report shows the top members of a user's network and the topics the user tweets about most. Free and paid versions are available:

    http://twitalyzer.com

Twitter Counter. Although Twitter Counter doesn't go into too much depth in measuring influence, the site provides an overview of a user's Twitter stats. It offers a historical graph of Twitter followers and provides predictions about when a user will reach certain follower benchmarks. The free site also allows users to compare their numbers with those of other Twitter users and see a chart of their follower growth:

    http://twittercounter.com

Follow the stars of
Return on Influence

Many of the stars discussed in this book are active on Twitter, sharing valuable content every day. Here are the Twitter handles of these Citizen Influencers, in order of appearance:

Lee Rainie	@lrainie
Sam Fiorella	@samfiorella
Valentina Monte	@valentinamonte
Naveen Krishnamurthy	@naveenk22
Calvin Lee	@mayhemstudios
Charles Dastodd	@dastodd
Nish Weiseth	@NishWeiseth
Amy Howell	@howellmarketing
Jessica Northey	@jessicanorthey
Robert Cialdini	@robertcialdini
Steve Farnsworth	@steveology
Jason Falls	@jasonfalls
Robert Scoble	@scobleizer
Danny Brown	@dannybrown
Geno Church	@genochurch
Jessica Turner	@jessicanturner
Jay Baer	@jaybaer
Michael Stelzner	@michael_stelzner
Tom Webster	@webby2001
Srivanos Rao	@skooloflife
John Falchetto	@johnfalchetto
Mark Harai	@mark_harai
Dino Dogan	@dino_dogan

Chris Brogan	@chrisbrogan
Mitch Joel	@mitchjoel
Gini Dietrich	@ginidietrich
Christopher S. Penn	@cspenn
Kelly Hancock	@nashvilleprov
Amie Marse	@content_money
Michael Brito	@britopian
Michelle Chmiliewski	@michmski
Shelly Kramer	@shellykramer
Nathan Dube	@dubiousmonk
Azeem Azhar	@azeem
Thomas Mickey	@thomasmickey
Joe Fernandez	@joefernandez
Kimmo Linkama	@kimmolinkama
Pam Moore	@pammktgnut
Matt Ridings	@techguerilla
Matt Owen	@lexx2009
Glen Gilmore	@glengilmore
Shripal Shah	@shrip1220
Jacob Varghese	@jacobvar
Neelu Modali	@nmodali
Pete Healy	@petehealy
Brandon Croke	@bcroke
Judith Samuels	@chieflemonhead
Beth Harte	@bethharte
Jon Buscall	@jonbuscall
Fergus Thomas	@fergpthomas
Paul Meyers	@thepaulmeyers
Helen Brown	@askhelenbrown
Dane Hartzell	@itsdane
Paul Saarinen	@taulpaul
David Rosen	@davidhrosen
Melissa Shymko	@melissashymko
Nate Riggs	@nateriggs
Stanford Smith	@pushingsocial
Laura Click	@lauraclick

References and Resources

3M in the United States. 2011. Available from http://solutions.3m.com.

Aakar. 2011. "Growth of Google Plus vs. Twitter vs. Facebook," Buzzom, http://www.buzzom.com/2011/07/growth-of-google-plus-vs-twitter-vs-facebook-stat/.

Anderson, Chris. 2009. *Free: The Future of a Radical Price.* Hyperion.

Baer, Jay. 2011. "5 Reasons Why Social Media Measurement Is Making You Lie to Yourself," http://www.convinceandconvert.com/social-media-measurement/5-reasons-social-media-measurement-is-making-you-lie-to-yourself/.

Baer, Jay. 2011. "9 Surprising New Facts about Social Media in America," http://www.convinceandconvert.com/social-media-research-2/9-surprising-new-facts-about-social-media-in-america/.

Baer, Jay, and Amber Naslund. 2011. *The Now Revolution.* Wiley.

Bajalad, Alec. 2011. "Klout CEO Joe Fernandez Wants to Measure Your Social Media Influence," BillBoard Biz, http://www.billboard.biz/bbbiz/industry/digital-and-mobile/klout-ceo-joe-fernandez-wants-to-measure-1005295302.story.

Base One Group. 2011 Blogosphere Report. *Base One.* Available from http://www.baseone.co.uk.

Benke, Andras. November 4, 2011. "The Life of a Tweet," Klout, Measuring Online Influence: The Official Klout Blog, http://corp.klout.com/blog/2011/11/the-life-of-a-tweet/.

Boorstin, Daniel. 1992. *The Image: A Guide to Pseudo-Events in America.* Vintage.

Brito, Michael. 2011. "3 Reasons Why Relevant Content Matters," Social Media Explorer, http://www.socialmediaexplorer.com/social-media-marketing/3-reasons-why-relevant-content-matters/.

Brogan, Chris. 2011. *Influencers,* http://www.chrisbrogan.com/influencers/.

Brogan, Chris, and Julien Smith. 2010. *Trust Agents: Using the Web to Build Influence, Improve Reputation and Earn Trust,* revised edition. Wiley.

Brown, Danny. 2011. "Make Yourself an Influencer by Playing the Klout +K Game," Insights, http://dannybrown.me/2011/06/26/make-yourself-an-influencer-by-playing-the-klout-k-game/.

Cha, Meeyoung, Hamed Haddadi, Fabricio Benevenuto, and Krishna P. Gummadi. 2010. "Measuring User Influence in Twitter: The Million

Follower Fallacy," *Artificial Intelligence*. Paper presented at Fourth Annual International AAAI Conference on Weblogs and Social Media (ICWSM), May 2010, Washington, D.C.

Chmiliewski, Michelle. May 2011. "Learn French in One Word," from *The Observing Participant*, http://observingparticipant.wordpress.com/2011/05/30/learn-french-in-one-word/.

Cialdini, Robert B. 2009. *Influence: The Psychology of Persuasion*, Kindle edition. HarperCollins.

Cordell, Greg, Geno Church, and Spike Jones. 2010. *Brains on Fire*. Wiley.

Delo, Cotton. November 2011. "Social-Influence Site Klout Partners with Brands to Distribute Freebies," *AdAge Digital*, http://adage.com/article/digital/freebies-klout-brand-partnerships-ftc/230756/.

Economist Staff. February 10, 2005. "Chief Humanising Officer." *The Economist*, http://www.economist.com/node/3644293.

E-Poll Market Research [database online]. Encino, CA, 2011, www.epollresearch.com.

Falls, Jason, and Erik Deckers. 2011. *No Bullshit Social Media*. Que.

Fernandez, Joe. November 13, 2011. "We Value Your Privacy," Klout, Measuring Online Influence: The Official Klout Blog, http://corp.klout.com/blog/2011/11/we-value-your-privacy/.

Fidelman, Mark. 2011. "Does Every Company Need a Robert Scoble?" http://www.cloudave.com/9246/does-every-company-need-a-robert-scoble-infographic-evangelism/.

Gale, Porter. 2011. "Hello, Klout. Meet Kred," Digital Next, New York, Crain Communications, http://adage.com/article/digitalnext/peoplebrowsr-launches-kred-competes-klout/230134/.

Garber, Megan. 2010. "Nicholas Christakis on the Networked Nature of Twitter," http://www.niemanlab.org/2010/12/nicholas-christakis-on-the-networked-nature-of-twitter/.

Gladwell, Malcolm. 2010. "Small Change: Why the Revolution Will Not Be Tweeted," *The New Yorker*.

Gladwell, Malcolm. 2000. *The Tipping Point: How Little Things Can Make a Big Difference*, rev. ed. Little, Brown.

Halvorson, Christina. 2009. *Content Strategy for the Web*. New Riders Press.

Handley, Ann, and C. C. Chapman. 2010. *Content Rules*. Wiley.

Hutchings, Emma. November 14, 2011. "Chevrolet Loans Out Its New Vehicle to People with Klout," PSFK: The Future of Retail, http://www.psfk.com/2011/11/chevrolet-loans-out-its-new-vehicle-to-people-with-klout.html#ixzz1dpmonR04.

Iyengar, Raghuram, Christopher Van den Bulte, and Jeonghye Choi. 2011. *Distinguishing among Mechanisms of Social Contagion in New Product Adoption*, Wharton School of the University of Pennsylvania.

http://marketing.wharton.upenn.edu/documents/research/
MultipleMechanisms.pdf.

Joel, Mitch. 2010. *Six Pixels of Separation*, reprint ed. Business Plus.

Kafka, Peter. September 26, 2011. "The Facebook Chart That Freaks
Google Out," *Wall Street Journal*, http://allthingsd.com/20110926/
the-facebook-chart-that-freaks-google-out/?mod=tweet.

Kirkpatrick, David, and David Sanger. 2011. "Egyptians and Tunisians
Collaborated to Shake Arab History," *New York Times,* section A,
http://www.nytimes.com/2011/02/14/world/middleeast/14egypt
-tunisia-protests.html?_r=3.

Kitano, Patrick. November 29, 2011. "Building Business Models Based on
Local Influence," *Street Fight Magazine,* http://streetfightmag.com/
2011/11/29/building-business-models-based-on-local-influence/

Le Roy Historical Society, Inc. 2011. Available from http://www
.jellogallery.org.

Local Response [database online]. Chelsea, NY, 2011, www.localresponse
.com.

Lynley, Matt. November 30, 2011. "Marc Benioff Is Convinced
Klout Will Save Your Business," *Business Insider,* http://www
.businessinsider.com/benioff-klout-radian6-update-2011
-11#ixzz1fPIIXbIA.

Marketing Evaluations, Inc. [database online]. Manhasset, NY, 2011,
www.qscores.com.

Mikkelson, Barbara. Snopes.com. "Post-it Note origin," 2011, http://
www.snopes.com/business/origins/post-it.asp.

Monaghan, Beth. 2011. "Joe Fernandez on Influence and Why It
Matters?"
Inklings, http://www.inkhouse.net/interview-with-klout%E2
%80%99s-joe-fernandez-on-influence-and-why-it-matters/.

Morris, Chris. 2011. "Followers for Sale: Buying Your Way to Twitter
Fame," Tech check, New York, http://www.cnbc.com/id/44005313.

Newman, Jared. 2011. "Cornell Software Learns How to Spot Fake
Online Reviews," Today @ PC World, *PC World*, http://www
.pcworld.com/article/236655/cornell_software_learns_how_to_spot
_fake_online_reviews.html.

Owen, Matt. 2010. "Why Klout Doesn't Count: Putting Social Media
Influence into Context," http://econsultancy.com/us/blog/6933-why
-klout-doesn-t-count-putting-social-media-influence-in-context.

Riggs, Nate. 2010. "7 Tips You Can Use to Improve Your Klout Score,"
Nate Riggs, Social Business Strategies, http://www.nateriggs
.com/2010/12/08/improve-klout-score-tips/content-marketing
-consulting.

Romero, Daniel M., Wojciech Goluba, Sitaram Asur, and Bernardo
A. Huberman. 2011. *Influence and Passivity in Social Media.* Paper

presented at ECML-PKDD 2011, September 2011, Athens, Greece. Part of this work has been published at WWW 2011.

Rothman, Joel. September 2011. "Does Klout Impact Conversions?" Revenue Marketing Blog, http://blog.eloqua.com/klout-and -conversions/.

Schaefer, Mark. 2010. "Finally! A B2B Social Media Success Story," Grow, http://www.businessesgrow.com/2009/10/19/finally-a-b2b -social-media-success-story/.

Schaefer, Mark. 2010. "Get Ready: Social Scoring Will Change Your Life," Grow, http://www.businessesgrow.com/2010/11/22/get-ready -social-scoring-will-change-your-life/.

Schaefer, Mark. 2011. "The Hidden Costs of Social Media Conversation," Grow, http://www.businessesgrow.com/2011/09/07/the-hidden-costs -of-social-media-conversation/.

Schaefer, Mark. 2011. "Let's Not Have a Quor-gasm," Grow, http://www .businessesgrow.com/2011/01/14/lets-not-have-a-quor-gasm/.

Schaefer, Mark. 2011. "McDonald's Scales to Meet Social Media Demands," Grow, http://www.businessesgrow.com/2011/03/15/ mcdonalds-scales-to-meet-social-media-demands-video/.

Schaefer, Mark. 2011. "Twitter, Klout and the Vacation Effect," Grow, http://www.businessesgrow.com/2011/06/18/twitter-klout-and-the -vacation-effect/.

Schaefer, Mark W. 2011. *The Tao of Twitter*. Knoxville, TN: self-published.

Scoble, Robert. 2010. "Is Quora the Biggest Blogging Innovation in 10 Years?" Scobleizer, http://scobleizer.com/2010/12/26/is-quora-the -biggest-blogging-innovation-in-10-years/.

Scoble, Robert. 2010. "Meet the Team That Knows Who Is Really Influential on Twitter (Klout)," http://scobleizer.com/2010/06/21 /meet-the-team-that-knows-who-is-really-influential-on-twitter -klout/.

Scoble, Robert. 2011. "Why I Was Wrong about Quora as a Blogging Service," http://scobleizer.com/2011/01/30/why-i-was-wrong-about -quora-as-a-blogging-service/.

Shapiro, Judy. 2011. "What's Klout's Pricing Model?" http://www.quora .com/Whats-Klouts-pricing-model.

Sherman, Ted. 2010. "History of Celebrity Endorsements," http://www .associatedcontent.com/article/2644371/history_of_celebrity _endorsements.html?cat=2.

Shiell, Andrea. 2011. "Klout, Tracking Political Clout on Twitter," Yeas and Nays, http://washingtonexaminer.com/blogs/yeas-nays/2011/07/ klout-tracking-political-clout-twitter#ixzz1Tp040NJd.

Solis, Brian. 2011. *Engage*. Wiley.

Steiner, Ina. 2011. "Addoway Reports the Power of Social Klout in Boosting Sales," E-commerce Bytes, http://www.auctionbytes.com/cab/abn/y11/m07/i26/s03.

Stelzner, Michael. 2011. *Launch: How to Propel Your Business Beyond the Competition.* Wiley.

Stock Lobster: Antique Stocks and Bonds. 2011. Available from http://www.stocklobster.com.

Subramanyam, Radha. 2011. "The Relationship Between Social Media Buzz and TV Ratings," NielsenWire, http://blog.nielsen.com/nielsenwire/online_mobile/the-relationship-between-social-media-buzz-and-tv-ratings/.

Teicher, David. 2010. "Need a Reservation? That Could Depend How Big You Are on Twitter (Really)," Digital Next, New York, Crain Communications, http://adage.com/article/digitalnext/marketing-las-vegas-palms-hotel-klout-scores/146189/.

Teitell, Beth. February 18, 2011. "The Ascent of the Social Media Climbers," *Boston Globe*, http://articles.boston.com/2011–02–18/business/29340198_1_credit-score-social-media-twitter.

Text Message Blog Staff. *USA Text Message Statistics.* Text message blog, http://www.textmessageblog.mobi/2009/02/19/text-message-statistics-usa/.

Trout, Robert. "John Winthrop and the Founding of the Massachusetts Bay Colony," http://east_west_dialogue.tripod.com/american_system/id14.html.

Turner, Catherine. 2011. "Publicis Partners with PeerIndex to Launch iHobo App," PR Newswire [database online], New York, www.prnewswire.com.

Webster, Thomas. "A True Measure of Influence," Brand Savant blog, http://brandsavant.com/a-true-measure-of-influence/.

Webster, Thomas. "A Call to Help New Zealand," Brand Savant blog, http://brandsavant.com/a-call-to-help-new-zealand/.

Weinberger, David, Christopher Locke, Rick Levine, Doc Searls, and Jake McKee. 2009. *The Cluetrain Manifesto,* 10th anniversary ed. Basic Books.

Wharton at Work. March 2009. "The Buzz Starts Here: Finding the First Mouth for Word-of-Mouth Marketing," http://knowledge.wharton.upenn.edu/article.cfm?articleid=2170.

Wong, Wailin. 2011. "Social Media Influence: Who Has Top Klout Scores in Chicago?" http://articles.chicagotribune.com/2011–04–30/business/ct-biz-0501-klout-20110430_1_social-media-twitter-influence.

Wong, Wailin. 2011. "Taking the Pulse of Social Media," *Chicago Tribune*, Lifestyle section, http://www.startribune.com/lifestyle/121584369.html?page=2&c=y.

Acknowledgments and Contributors to the Book

Obviously this book was built on the cumulative wisdom and insight of dozens of amazing people. That's the only way to cover an entirely new subject like this.

At the top of the list of people I owe deeply are the dozens of true influencers who contributed their minds and time through the interviews I completed for this book. Most of them did it without really knowing me; they were simply interested in the topic and, in the very best spirit of the social web, just wanted to help. It would be tedious to mention all the people already prominently featured in this book and the more than 100 folks who were interviewed, but let's just say I will be on the "delivery" end of reciprocity for years to come! I owe special gratitude to Dr. Robert Cialdini, who not only allowed me to dissect his wonderful weapons of influence theory in the context of online power but encouraged me to do it.

Thanks also to the team at Klout, especially CEO Joe Fernandez, for opening up the story of their company for the world. There were no guarantees—they didn't know how this book would turn out— yet they generously gave me exclusive access to their inner workings so that this story could be told. Whether you love Klout the company or hate it, I hope you have come to admire the guts, dedication, and authenticity of the people behind the scenes.

I had two extraordinary special contributors to this book who deserve your applause and my thanks: Stanford Smith and Laura Click.

Stanford Smith contributed research and writing toward the extremely challenging story, told in Chapter 5, of the history of influence marketing. Stanford is the vice president of marketing at Fluency Media, a full-service interactive agency whose clients include fast-growing technology start-ups, government agencies, nonprofit organizations, and Fortune 500 companies. Stanford is also the founder of the popular blog *PushingSocial.com*, a leading voice and resource for busy professionals who are using social media to transform their personal brands and business.

Laura Click wrote Appendix A on social media basics as well as the company profiles in Appendix B. As Laura focused on these important details that made the book more useful and complete, I could focus on the bigger picture and the more strategic elements of the book. Laura is the founder and chief innovator at Blue Kite Marketing, a consulting group focused on helping small service-based businesses reach new heights. Throughout her 10-year career as a marketing and public relations professional, Laura has developed successful campaigns for Fortune 500 companies, small businesses, nonprofits, and government agencies. Laura blogs at www.fly bluekite.com.

Every word of every interview was transcribed from an audio file to text by Rebecca Schaefer, the world's greatest wife. This effort was a heroic one that had an important and unanticipated side benefit. As my wife became immersed in these conversations, she became a bit of an expert in the subject herself—and a valued confidant and advisor.

My dear friend and virtual assistant Carrie Bond helped with fundamental research on the companies and personalities featured in this book. Brian Ellis, the founder of Knoxville's Anocial Social Media, contributed critical insights to the section of the book that explored the underbelly of social media cheating. Trusted intern and future social media expert Brittany Shaffer cranked out fact checking and additional research with lightning speed. My friend Annette Penny of Toronto's Inspire and Acquire agency provided valuable insight and support through her selfless proofreading.

Many people declare traditional publishing dead. Don't tell my senior editor Stephanie Frerich and the folks at McGraw-Hill. We need books. We need publishers. I would not have been able to create *Return on Influence* without them.

My friends at VIEO Design created the book's website and other digital properties. You can visit them at www.vieodesign.com.

Atlanta-based MLT Creative, an inspiring B2B marketing agency, has been a valued business partner and collaborator for years. The MLT design team is responsible for putting together some of the collateral material to support this publication, including an e-book and slides for my speech. Visit MLT at www.mltcreative.com.

Joe Atkins is the miracle worker who made me look presentable in photos for the book design and website. Check out his work at www.jophotoonline.com.

Thanks to Kacy Maxwell for the hilarious Klout cartoon at the top of this section. Kacy regularly contributes social media cartoons to my blog at www.businessesGROW.com.

I couldn't finish a book like this without thanking the thousands of people who encourage and challenge me every single day on the social web through their tweets, blog comments, and other generous expressions of support. The *{grow}* community is real. The Citizen Influencer is my story and their story, too. My influence was not granted to me by inherited wealth, political appointment, or athletic prowess. It was earned every day, not the old-fashioned way but the new way, through the creation of content and the blessings of people who decided it was worth moving around the web. Thank you so very, very much!

Most important, I thank God for His patience with this broken servant and for granting me the opportunity to glorify Him through this work.

Mark W. Schaefer

INDEX

A

Activism, 120–122
Addoway, 142
Adele, 123
Advocacy, 135–136, 142–143
Alden, Jim, 142–143
Algorithms:
  Klout score, 107, 111, 153–158,
    168
  marketing, 89–90
  protecting, 117–118
Allen, Gracie, 83
Amplification probability, 155
Anderson, Chris, 45
Anti-Klout frenzy (2011), 111–112
Application programming inter-
    face (API), 97n.1
Arab Spring of 2011, 121
Ash, Mary Kay, 87–88, 91
Asur, Sitaram, 156–157
@replies, 185
Audi, 132, 138, 142–143
Audience, size of, 71–73
Audio content, 67
Augmented reality, 175
Authority, 32–37, 50–52, 56–57
Autoresponse, 22–28, 33–34, 36
Avatars, 185
Azhar, Azeem, 91–92, 169–171,
    196

B

B2B applications of Klout,
    146–147
Babbit, B.T., 85–86

BackTweets, 189
Baer, Jay, 50, 51, 56, 59, 195
Barnum, P.T., 83
Barrymore, Ethel, 87
Base One, 34
Baudrillard, Jean, 126
Beauty by Mary Kay, 88
Benevenuto, Fabricio, 166
Benny, Jack, 87
Bieber, Justin, 98, 124
Black, Rebecca, 123, 159
Black hat, 73n.2
BlackBerry, 133
Bloggers, 14, 34, 36
Blogs, 184
  content for, 65–66
  epidemics of influence from,
    26–27
  FTC regulation on, 150, 151
  improving your Klout score
    with, 162, 163
  preservation of, 37–38
Bolin Marketing, 145–147
Boorstin, Daniel, 75
Booshaka, 189
Bots, Klout scores of, 113–114
Brains on Fire Agency, 34
Brand Savant (Tom Webster), 119
Brands, buffers for, 137–138
Brito, Michael, 76–78, 196
Broadband communication, viii
Brogan, Chris, 46, 60–61, 64, 196
Brown, Danny, 33, 34, 123, 195
Brown, Helen, 143–144, 196
Brown, Rebel, 63
Burns, George, 83

About the Author

Mark W. Schaefer is a father, husband, and faculty member at Rutgers University with 30 years of experience in sales, public relations, and international marketing. He is the founder and executive director of Schaefer Marketing Solutions, a U.S.-based marketing consulting firm, and a globally recognized speaker and blogger. Mark has advanced degrees in both marketing and applied behavioral sciences and is also the author of *The Tao of Twitter*.

Follow his blog {grow} at www.businessesgrow.com/blog.

On Twitter, he can be found at @markwschaefer.

Continue the conversation on social media, influence, and social scoring at the book's website, www.ReturnOnInfluence.com.